高校英语选修课系列教材

INTERCULTURAL COMMUNICATION
AN ENGLISH READING COURSEBOOK

跨文化交际英语阅读教程

主　编　李　晓
副主编　许学燕
编　者　李　萌　任　喆　郑庆庆

清华大学出版社
北　京

内 容 简 介

本书基于内容和语言融合教学理念，以英语语言为载体，以立德树人为导向，以跨文化交际意识和能力培养为目标进行教学设计。本书共 10 个单元，每个单元包括两篇跨文化交际阅读文章、若干文化知识拓展及两个主题案例分析。各单元以文本阅读为主线，涵盖跨文化交际的基础理论、交际过程与实践应用等方面，旨在引导学生理解、尊重、包容世界多元文化，拓展其国际视野。阅读文本后配有形式多样的练习题，以提高学生的语言综合运用能力和跨文化交际能力。本书为"线上 + 线下"相结合的新形态教材，每个单元的 Text B 部分为线上学习，充分赋能教师的混合式教学实践，增强学生的自主学习能力。

本书的读者对象为普通高校修读相关课程的本科生，以及致力于提升英语跨文化读写能力的大众读者。

版权所有，侵权必究。举报：010-62782989，beiqinquan@tup.tsinghua.edu.cn。

图书在版编目（CIP）数据

跨文化交际英语阅读教程/李晓主编. —北京：清华大学出版社，2023.12（2024.9 重印）
高校英语选修课系列教材
ISBN 978-7-302-64198-8

Ⅰ.①跨⋯　Ⅱ.①李⋯　Ⅲ.①英语—阅读教学—高等学校—教材　Ⅳ.① H319.37

中国国家版本馆 CIP 数据核字（2023）第 135319 号

责任编辑：许玲玉
封面设计：子　一
责任校对：王凤芝
责任印制：丛怀宇

出版发行：清华大学出版社
　　网　　址：https://www.tup.com.cn, https://www.wqxuetang.com
　　地　　址：北京清华大学学研大厦 A 座　　**邮　编**：100084
　　社 总 机：010-83470000　　**邮　购**：010-62786544
　　投稿与读者服务：010-62776969, c-service@tup.tsinghua.edu.cn
　　质量反馈：010-62772015, zhiliang@tup.tsinghua.edu.cn
印 装 者：三河市人民印务有限公司
经　　销：全国新华书店
开　　本：185mm×260mm　　**印　张**：13　　**字　数**：271 千字
版　　次：2023 年 12 月第 1 版　　**印　次**：2024 年 9 月第 2 次印刷
定　　价：62.00 元

产品编号：100534-01

前　言

　　从早期部落间的接触到如今全球化时代下的交流互鉴，跨文化交际在人类历史发展的进程中从未停止。Hall（1959）说，文化与交际密不可分，文化即交际，交际即文化。有人类就有文化，有不同地域、民族、种族和国度就有不同文化。不同文化在历史发展的长河中，常常发生对立、冲突，甚至战争，但对立、冲突往往是短暂的，文明互鉴、文化交融才是主流。

　　当前，人类社会正处在一个大发展、大变革、大调整时期。各国相互联系、相互依存的程度空前加深，人类已经成为你中有我、我中有你的命运共同体。任何人、任何国家都无法独善其身，唯有通过平等的跨文化交流与对话，才能实现共赢共享，促进人类的可持续发展。如何高效地与来自不同文化背景的人进行交流、如何提高跨文化交际能力，是当今社会向每个公民提出的时代课题。

　　面对世界百年未有之大变局，我国亟须培养大批既有家国情怀，又有国际视野的国际化人才。《教育部等八部门关于加快和扩大新时代教育对外开放的意见》（2020年）明确提出要"提升我国高等教育人才培养的国际竞争力，加快培养具有全球视野的高层次国际化人才"。在此背景下，近年来，国内跨文化交际研究与教学迅速发展，开设这一课程的院校越来越多，涉及学科专业越来越广，对高质量教材的需求也越来越强。基于此，我们组织、策划编写了这本《跨文化交际英语阅读教程》，以期为新时代复合型人才培养贡献力量。

编写理念

　　《跨文化交际英语阅读教程》基于内容和语言融合（Content and Language Integrated Learning, CLIL）教学理念，以英语语言为载体，以立德树人为导向，以跨文化交际意识和能力培养为目标进行教学设计、内容选择和板块构建。本教材旨在引导学生关注和思考人类面临的共同问题和挑战，帮助其识别、理解、尊重、包容世界多元文化，拓宽国际视野，辩证看待文化差异；在中外文化对比的基础上，加深对中华文化的理解和认同，增强文化自信和民族自豪感，提高语言综合运用能力和跨文化交际能力。

跨文化交际英语阅读教程
Intercultural Communication: An English Reading Coursebook

教材特色

1. 遵循 CLIL 教学理念，将跨文化交际理论与实践密切融合

教材基于内容和语言融合教学理念进行教学设计，以跨文化交际学科知识为内容，旨在培养学生掌握跨文化交际基本概念、主要理论的同时又能较好地运用英语进行跨文化沟通，实现专业知识和语言能力的交互提升。

2. 选材内容丰富，结构明晰，课堂可操作性强

各单元均由开篇名言、学习目标、单元导读、文本阅读、知识拓展、案例分析等部分构成，结构科学合理，符合学生渐进习得之规律。阅读文本多选自跨文化交际著作名篇、学术及报刊文章，语料真实生动；文本后精心设计了相映成趣的练习活动，课堂教学可操作性强。

3. 落实立德树人，将课程思政自然融入教学内容

教材在内容选择上将中国优秀文化自然融入，引导学生在对比中外文化的基础上，加深对中华文化的理解和认同，增强文化自信和民族自豪感，关注和思考人类面临的共同问题和挑战。

4. "线上 + 线下"资源共建，赋能混合式教学实践

为促进学生自主学习，保证同伴评估、讨论及教师反馈的即时性，本教材打破纸介质传播载体的局限，同步配备网络学习平台。平台具备教学管理功能，便于教师更加自如地开展混合式教学实践、更加有效地参与及辅助学生的学习过程。

教材结构

本教材共 10 个单元，涉及跨文化交际的必要性、交际与文化、感知与文化、跨文化交际障碍、跨文化身份认同、跨文化价值取向、言语交际与文化、非言语交际与文化、跨文化冲突管理、文化适应等，涵盖跨文化交际的基础理论、交际过程与实践应用等各个方面。各单元均以文本阅读为主线，配有名言警句、词汇表、形式多样的练习和案例分析，同时还提供了较丰富的主题文化拓展知识，以满足多样化的教学情境和需求。

教材各单元结构如下：

1. Lead-in

以跨文化交际小故事引出问题或现象，点明单元主题，旨在启发学生思考跨文化的相关问题与要点，增强跨文化意识与敏感性。

2. Text A

Text A 为理论篇，选材于国内外跨文化交际经典著作，旨在让学生了解跨文化交际的基本概念、理论、知识、技巧。每篇阅读文本后配有文化注释、词汇表等资源和练

习，方便学生扫清阅读障碍，加深对文本的理解与掌握，提高语言综合运用能力。

3. Expanding Intercultural Knowledge

该板块是对单元主题的拓展和延伸，学生通过阅读文本，完成反思和讨论问题，从而加深对跨文化交际核心概念的理解，提高语言表达和应用能力。

4. Text B

Text B 为实践篇，材料多选自名人演讲、国内外报纸杂志或网站文章等，旨在引导学生理论联系实际，将跨文化交际知识、理论与现实世界进行联结。每篇阅读文本后配有文化注释、词汇表等资源和练习。此部分内容在"清华社英语在线"数字化互动教学平台上呈现。

5. Case Study

该板块的案例同样选自国内外跨文化交际经典著作，内容贴合单元主题，语境丰富，涵盖了跨文化交际学科重要知识点，生动形象地展示了跨文化交际过程中许多复杂和矛盾的问题。问题设置由点及面，旨在帮助学生运用单元所学理论，发现、分析并解决语境中的交际问题。

编写团队的各位教师均有海外学习或工作的经历，在英语语言教学、跨文化交际教学及跨文化人才培养方面都具有丰富的经验。他们为本教材的顺利编写付出了辛勤努力。湖北中医药大学澳大利亚籍语言教师 Glenn. A. Bolas 对教材语言进行了润色和校对，在此表示感谢。

本教材是湖北大学本科生院 2022 年度教学改革研究项目的成果之一；同时，教材出版也获得湖北大学教材经费资助项目和湖北大学曼城联合学院的资助，一并致谢。

教材在编写过程中参考了大量资料，特在书末统列为参考文献，并就此对这些资料的创作者表示衷心的感谢。清华大学出版社杨文娟、许玲玉和曹诗悦三位编辑对本教材的出版给予了大力支持，在此表示诚挚谢意。

由于编写时间和编者水平有限，本教材难免有疏漏。敬请专家、读者批评指正，以便我们不断改进提高。

李 晓

于武汉沙湖之滨

2023 年 2 月

Contents

Unit 1 **Imperatives for Intercultural Communication** 1
    Lead-in   The Roads Linking the East with the West 2
    Text A   Why Study Intercultural Communication? 3
    Expanding Intercultural Knowledge 16
    Text B   Work Together to Build the Silk Road Economic Belt and the 21st Century Maritime Silk Road 18
    Case Study 19

Unit 2 **Communication and Culture** 21
    Lead-in   A Monkey Exploring the Great World 22
    Text A   Communication and Culture: The Voice and the Echo 23
    Expanding Intercultural Knowledge 34
    Text B   Questions of Culture 37
    Case Study 38

Unit 3 **Perception and Culture** 41
    Lead-in   Gift 42
    Text A   Becoming a Sensitive Intercultural Perceiver 43
    Expanding Intercultural Knowledge 52

v

Text B How Ten Years in China Changed Me Forever 58
Case Study 59

Unit 4 Barriers to Intercultural Communication 61

Lead-in How to Get Them to Jump? 62
Text A Barriers to Effective Intercultural Communication 63
Expanding Intercultural Knowledge 74
Text B Increasing Racial Discrimination Against Asians Exposes Overall Racist Nature of U.S. Society 77
Case Study 78

Unit 5 Identity and Culture 81

Lead-in Who Am I? 82
Text A Cultural Identity: Issues of Belonging 83
Expanding Intercultural Knowledge 93
Text B I Am Not Your Asian Stereotype 94
Case Study 95

Unit 6 Cultural Values 97

Lead-in Proverbs and Values 98
Text A Values and Value Orientations Across Cultures 99
Expanding Intercultural Knowledge 110
Text B Eastern vs. Western Parenting 112
Case Study 113

Unit 7 Language and Culture 115

Lead-in Eastern vs. Western Verbal Styles 116
Text A The Connection Between Language and Culture 117
Expanding Intercultural Knowledge 127
Text B How Language Shapes the Way We Think 129
Case Study 130

Contents

Unit 8　Nonverbal Communication and Culture..................................133
　　Lead-in　Obama's Bow in Japan 134
　　Text A　The Silent Language 135
　　Expanding Intercultural Knowledge 144
　　Text B　Understanding Personal Space Across Cultures 147
　　Case Study.. 148

Unit 9　Intercultural Conflict Management 151
　　Lead-in　What Would You Do?... 152
　　Text A　Culture, Communication and Conflict 153
　　Expanding Intercultural Knowledge 163
　　Text B　How and Why Does Conflict Occur? 166
　　Case Study.. 167

Unit 10　Intercultural Adaptation...................... 169
　　Lead-in　Doubts 170
　　Text A　Adapting to a New Culture....................................... 171
　　Expanding Intercultural Knowledge 182
　　Text B　Don't Be Afraid of Being Vulnerable 187
　　Case Study.. 188

References 191

"清华社英语在线"（TUP English Online）平台使用指南................... 195

Unit 1
Imperatives for Intercultural Communication

Today, after more than a century of electric technology, we have extended our central nervous systems itself in a global embrace, abolishing both space and time as far as our planet is concerned.

—*Marshall McLuhan*

历史告诉我们：文明在开放中发展，民族在融合中共存。

——习近平

Learning Objectives

Upon completion of this unit, you will be able to:

- Appreciate the importance of studying intercultural communication.
- Define such terms as *globalization*, *global village* and *ethnocentrism*.
- Understand how a community is formed.
- Understand the historical background and significance of the Belt and Road Initiative.

 Lead-in

The Roads Linking the East with the West

Reference to the "Silk Road" often conjures up（联想到）a Hollywood-based romantic image of caravans（旅行队）transporting exotic goods across Central Asia between China and the West. In actuality, however, there were numerous roads, or routes, linking China with the West, beginning late in the first millennium（千年）B.C. and lasting until the fifteenth century A.D. These tracks passed through Central Asia, South Asia, along the coast of the Arabian Peninsula（阿拉伯半岛）, and through today's Middle East. In addition to the many tradesmen, the routes were traveled by explorers, religious prelates（教士）, philosophers, warriors, and foreign emissaries. New products, art works, technologies, innovations, and philosophical ideas traveled in both directions to consumers in the East and West, as well as those in between. These overland conduits（通道）passed through the domains（疆域）of many different cultures. Thus, a successful transit（通行）requires the knowledge and ability to effectively interact with peoples instilled with contrasting worldviews, possessing varied cultural values, and speaking a multiplicity of languages.

(Source: Larry A. Samovar et al., *Intercultural Communication: A Reader*)

Unit 1 Imperatives for Intercultural Communication

Questions for Intercultural Understanding

1. Who traveled the routes of the "Silk Road"? What made the roads prosperous?

2. What difficulties or challenges might those travelers encounter while interacting with people from different cultures? How could they overcome these problems and difficulties?

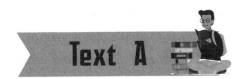

Why Study Intercultural Communication?

1   With rapid changes in the global economy, technology, transportation systems, and **immigration** policies, the world is becoming a small, **intersecting community**. We find ourselves having increased contact with people who are culturally different. In a global workforce, people bring with them different work habits and cultural practices. For example, cultural strangers may **approach** problem-solving tasks or **nonverbal** emotional expression **issues** differently. They may develop friendships and romantic relationships with different expectations and rhythms. They may also have different communication desires, end goals, and **emphases** in an intercultural **encounter**. In this twenty-first century global world, people are **constantly** moving across borders, into and out of a country. Neighborhoods and communities are changing. In what was once a **homogeneous** community, we may now find more **diversity** and cultural values **in flux**.

2   The study of intercultural communication is about the study of communication that **involves**, at least in part, cultural group membership differences. It is about **acquiring** the necessary knowledge and dynamic skills to manage such differences appropriately and effectively. It is also about developing a creative **mindset** to see things from different angles without **rigid** prejudgment. There are indeed many practical reasons for studying intercultural communication.

Fostering Global Peace

3   The need for global peace has never been more **apparent**. The key issue is

this: Can individuals of different sexes, ages, **ethnicities**, races, languages, and religions peacefully coexist on the planet? The history of humankind is hardly grounds for optimism. Contact among different national groups—from the earliest civilizations until today—often leads to **disharmony**.

4   To practice global peacemaking, we must hold a firm **commitment** that considerations of fairness should apply to all identity groups. We must be willing to consider sharing economic and social resources with **underprivileged** groups to **level** the fear and **resentment** factors. We must start practicing win-win **collaborative** dialogs with individuals or groups we may currently consider our enemies. We must **display** a *mindful listening*[1] attitude even if we do not like the individuals or agree with their ideas or viewpoints. In displaying our respect for other nations or groups of individuals, we may open doors for more dialogs and deeper contacts. Human respect is a **prerequisite** for any type or form of intercultural or interethnic communication.

Adjusting to Globalization of Economy

5   You may want to know more about intercultural communication because you **foresee** tremendous changes in the workplace. This is one important reason to know about other cultures and communication patterns. In addition, knowing about intercultural communication is **strategically** important for a nation's businesses in the emerging transnational economy. As noted by writer Carol Hymowitz of *The Wall Street Journal*[2], "If companies are going to sell products and services globally, then they will need a rich mix of employees with varied **perspectives** and experiences. They will need top **executives** who understand different countries and cultures."

A. Global Economy

6   Businesses all around the world are continually expanding into overseas markets in a process of *globalization*[3]. The world economy has become globally interdependent. This trend towards a global economy brings people and products together from around the world.

7   In the face of economic globalization, nations must determine how to remain competitive and must find ways to **promote** products and services in the international market. This interdependence between economies of different nations increases the need for effective intercultural communication and **calls**

Unit 1   Imperatives for Intercultural Communication

for ever more skillful interaction in the future across linguistic and national boundaries.

B. Workforce Heterogeneity

8   In this global age, it is **inevitable** that employees and customers from dissimilar cultures are in constant contact with one another—whether it is through face-to-face, cellular phone, Skype, smartphone, or e-mail contacts. Workplace **heterogeneity** on the global level represents both opportunities and challenges to individuals and organizations.

9   Global managers and employees, international human resource groups, global product development teams, multiethnic customer service groups, and international marketing and sales teams can all benefit from mastering intercultural communication competencies. Any groups or individuals that must communicate **on a daily basis** with culturally diverse coworkers, clients, or customers can **reap the rewards of** acquiring the awareness, knowledge, and skills of **flexible** intercultural communication. Intercultural communication knowledge and skills are needed to solve problems, manage **conflicts**, and **forge** new **visions** on both global and **domestic** levels.

Multicultural work environments are becoming increasingly common. Given this trend, workers need to learn to deal with cultural differences.

Engaging in Creative Multicultural Problem Solving

10   Our ability to value different approaches to problem solving and mindfully move away from traditional "either/or" **binary** thinking can expand diverse options in managing team intercultural problems. We learn more from people who are different from us than from those who are similar to us.

11   Research findings indicate the quality of ideas produced in ethnically diverse groups has been **rated** significantly higher by experts than that in ethnically homogeneous groups. Of course, culturally heterogeneous teams also have more conflicts or communication struggles than homogeneous work teams. However, if such conflicts are managed **competently** and flexibly, the outcome of heterogeneous team **negotiations** often results in a better-quality product than that produced by a homogeneous team. Losing a **vital** employee with significant ties to a multicultural or diverse community can cost many missed business opportunities and fruitful outcomes.

Comprehending the Role of Technology in Global Communication

12   In the 1960s, media **guru** Marshall McLuhan[4] **coined** the term *global village* to describe a world in which communication technology, such as TV, radio, and news services, brings news and information to the most remote parts of the world. Today people are connected through e-mails, websites, and social media on the Internet. The Internet is the central **hub**—the channel that offers us a wide-open space to communicate globally and to connect with individuals from **diverse walks of life**.

13   In this twenty-first century, both individualists[5] and collectivists[6], regardless of what cultures they are from, are at a crossroads of **redefining**, exploring, and reinventing their identities. On a global scale, new generations of individuals are attempting to create a third identity—a **hybrid** identity that **fuses** the global and local cultures together. This global connection is so **appealing**, and so persuasive, that it constantly shapes and makes us reexamine who we are or what we want to become. Technology allows us to develop relationships across the **barriers** of time, space, geography, and cultural ethnic boundaries.

Deepening Self-Awareness and Other-Awareness

14   One of the most important reasons for studying intercultural communication is to **gain an awareness of** one's own cultural identity and background. We acquire our cultural beliefs, values, and communication **norms** often on a very **unconscious** level. Without a comparative basis, we may never question the way we have been conditioned and socialized in our primary cultural system. Cultural socialization, in one sense, encourages the development of *ethnocentrism*.

Unit 1 Imperatives for Intercultural Communication

Ethnocentrism means seeing our own culture as the center of the universe and seeing other cultures as insignificant or even **inferior**.

15 Without sound comparative cross-cultural knowledge, we may look at the world from only one **lens**—that is, our own cultural lens. With a **solid** intercultural knowledge base, we may begin to understand the possible value differences and similarities between our own cultural system and that of another cultural system. We may be able to explain why people behave the way they do from their culture's logic systems or value patterns.

(Source: Stella Ting-Toomey & Leeva C. Chung, *Understanding Intercultural Communication*, Chapter 1)

New Words

acquire	*v.*	to gain sth. by your own efforts, ability or behavior 获得，得到
apparent	*adj.*	easy to see or understand 显而易见的
appealing	*adj.*	attractive or interesting 有吸引力的，有感染力的
approach	*v.*	to start dealing with a problem, task, etc. in a particular way 着手处理
barrier	*n.*	a problem, rule or situation that prevents sb. from doing sth., or that makes sth. impossible 障碍；阻力；关卡
binary	*adj.*	consisting of two things or parts 二元的
coin	*v.*	to invent a new word or phrase that other people then begin to use 创造
collaborative	*adj.*	involving, or done by, several people or groups of people working together 合作的，协作的，协力的
commitment	*n.*	a promise to do sth. or to behave in a particular way; a promise to support sb./sth.; the fact of committing oneself 承诺，许诺，允诺

community	n.	all the people who live in a particular area, country, etc. 社团，社群
competently	adv.	a way that shows enough skill or knowledge to do something well or to the necessary standard 足以胜任地，有能力地，称职地
conflict	n.	a situation in which people, groups or countries are involved in a serious disagreement or argument 冲突；争执，争论
constantly	adv.	all the time; repeatedly 一直；重复不断地
disharmony	n.	a lack of agreement about important things, which causes bad feelings between people or groups of people 不协调；不和谐
display	v.	to put sth. in a place where people can see it easily; to show sth. to people 陈列，展出，展示
diversity	n.	a range of many people or things that are very different from each other 差异（性），不同（点）
domestic	adj.	relating to a person's own country 国内的，本土的
emphases	n.	(pl. of emphasis) special importance that is given to sth. 重点
encounter	n.	a meeting, especially one that is sudden, unexpected or violent（意外、突然或暴力的）相遇，邂逅，遭遇
ethnicity	n.	the fact of belonging to a particular race 种族渊源，种族特点
executive	n.	a person who has an important job as a manager of a company or an organization（公司或机构的）经理，主管领导，管理人员
flexible	adj.	able to change to suit new conditions or situations 能适应新情况的，灵活的，可变动的
foresee	v.	to think sth. is going to happen in the future; to know about sth. before it happens 预料，预见，预知

Unit 1 Imperatives for Intercultural Communication

forge	*v.*	to form or bring into being especially by an expenditure of efforts 努力建成，形成
foster	*v.*	to encourage sth. to develop 促进；助长；培养
fuse	*v.*	to combine or be combined together（使）融合
guru	*n.*	a person who is an expert on a particular subject or who is very good at doing sth. 专家，权威，大师
heterogeneity	*n.*	the quality of being diverse and not comparable in kind 异质性
homogeneous	*adj.*	consisting of things or people that are all the same or all of the same type 由相同（或同类型）事物（或人）组成的，同种类的
hub	*n.*	the central and most important part of a particular place or activity（某地或活动的）中心，核心
hybrid	*adj.*	made up of different aspects or components 混合的
immigration	*n.*	the process of coming to live permanently in a country that is not your own; the number of people who do this 移民；移居
inevitable	*adj.*	certain to happen and unable to be avoided or prevented 不可避免的，不能防止的
inferior	*adj.*	not good or not as good as sb./sth. else 较差的，次的
intersecting	*adj.*	meeting or crossing each other 相交的，交叉的
involve	*v.*	to have or include as a necessary part, element, or circumstance 包含；需要
issue	*n.*	a problem or worry that sb. has with sth.（有关某事的）问题，担忧
lens	*n.*	a curved piece of glass or plastic that makes things look larger, smaller or clearer when you look through it 透镜；镜片
level	*v.*	to make sth. equal or similar 使相等，使平等，使相似

mindset	n.	a set of attitudes or fixed ideas that sb. has and that are often difficult to change 观念模式，思维倾向
negotiation	n.	formal discussion between people who are trying to reach an agreement 谈判，磋商，协商
nonverbal	adj.	things such as the expression on your face, your arm movements, or your tone of voice, which show how you feel about sth. without using words 不用语言表达的
norm	n.	standards of behavior that are typical of or accepted within a particular group or society 规范，行为标准
perspective	n.	a particular attitude towards sth.; a way of thinking about sth. 态度，观点，思考方法
prerequisite	n.	sth. that must exist or happen before sth. else can happen or be done 先决条件，前提，必备条件
promote	v.	to help sth. to happen or develop 促进，提升
rate	v.	to have or think that sb./sth. has a particular level of quality, value, etc. 评估，评价，估价
redefine	v.	to change the nature or limits of sth.; to make people consider sth. in a new way 改变……的本质（或界限）；重新定义；使重新考虑
resentment	n.	a feeling of anger or unhappiness about sth. that you think is unfair 愤恨，怨恨
rigid	adj.	very strict and difficult to change 死板的；僵硬的
solid	adj.	having a strong basis 可靠的，可信赖的
strategically	adv.	in a way that is meant to achieve a particular purpose or to gain an advantage 根据全局而安排地，战略性地
unconscious	adj.	(of feelings, thoughts, etc.) existing or happening without your realizing or being aware; not deliberate or controlled 无意识的；自然流露的

underprivileged	*adj.*	having less money and fewer opportunities than most people in society 在社会中处于弱势的；贫苦的；机遇少的；底层的
vision	*n.*	the ability to think about or plan the future with great imagination and intelligence 想象力；眼力，远见卓识
vital	*adj.*	necessary or essential in order for sth. to succeed or exist 必不可少的，对……极重要的

Useful Expressions

call for	to demand of; to support sth. publicly 需要；提倡
diverse walks of life	different industries, professions and trades 各行各业
gain an awareness of	to get to know that sth. exists and is important 获得……的意识，认识到
in flux	constantly changing 不断变化
on a daily basis	daily, everyday 每天
reap the rewards of	to get sth. because you have behaved well, worked hard, or provided a service to the community 收获……的回报

Cultural Notes

1. mindful listening

Mindful listening is a way of listening without judgement, criticism, or interruption.

2. *The Wall Street Journal*

The Wall Street Journal is an American business-focused, international daily newspaper based in New York City, with international editions also available in Chinese and Japanese. The Journal, along with its Asian editions, is published six days a week by Dow Jones & Company, a division of News Corp.

3. globalization

Globalization is a term used to describe the increasing connectedness and interdependence of world cultures and economies.

4. Marshall McLuhan

Marshall McLuhan (1911–1980), a Canadian medium study scholar, was the first person to popularize the concept of "global village" and to consider its social effects. His insights were revolutionary at the time, and fundamentally changed how everyone has thought about media, technology, and communications ever since. McLuhan chose the insightful phrase "global village" to highlight his observation that an electronic nervous system (the media) was rapidly integrating the planet—events in one part of the world would be experienced in other parts in real time.

5. individualists

Individualists are those who advocate and practice individualism (个体主义). Individualistic cultures emphasize personal rights and responsibilities, privacy, voicing one's own opinion, freedom, innovation and self-expression.

6. collectivists

Collectivists are those who advocate and practice collectivism (集体主义). Collectivistic cultures emphasize community, collaboration, shared interest, harmony, tradition, the public good, and maintaining face.

Reading Comprehension

I. **Choose the best options to answer the following questions or fill in the blanks.**

1. What's the text mainly about?
   A. The importance of promoting global peace.
   B. The approaches to creative multicultural problem thinking.
   C. The practical reasons for learning intercultural communication.
   D. The importance of the awareness of cultural identity.

2. According to the text, which of the following is mentioned as a reason for studying intercultural communication?
   A. To adjust to the globalization of economy.
   B. To be more engaged in creative multicultural problem solving.
   C. To gain deep self-awareness and other-awareness.
   D. All of the above.

3. What is identified as a key issue for fostering global peace as mentioned in the text?
   A. Disharmony among different national groups.
   B. The peaceful coexistence of individuals with cultural differences.

Unit 1 Imperatives for Intercultural Communication

   C. The history of humankind.

   D. The need for rapid changes in the global economy.

4. Which of the following statements about "mindful listening" in Paragraph 4 is the author most likely to agree with?

   A. It is associated with a commitment to the fairness among all identity groups.

   B. It indicates an attitude without judgement, criticism or interruption when confronted with different ideas or viewpoints.

   C. It refers to a shared responsibility of using economic and social resources with underprivileged groups.

   D. It refers to an ability to initiate collaborative dialogs despite of divergence.

5. The author mentions the quote by Carol Hymowitz of *The Wall Street Journal* in Paragraph 5 to _____.

   A. stress the ability to foresee tremendous changes in workplace

   B. illustrate the strategic importance of intercultural communication

   C. highlight the vital role of top executives in global companies

   D. emphasize the importance of expanding the global market

6. It can be inferred from the text that _____.

   A. the quality of ideas produced in heterogeneous groups are of less value than that in ethnically homogeneous groups

   B. there tends to be more conflicts and divergence in ethnically homogeneous groups than in ethnically diverse groups

   C. the negotiations of the heterogeneous team are bound to (注定) produce better results than those of a homogeneous team

   D. an employee with significant connections to a multicultural community could bring more business opportunities and fruitful outcomes

7. According to the author, the term "ethnocentrism" in Paragraph 14 refers to a tendency of seeing one's own culture _____ others.

   A. superior to   B. inferior to

   C. as significant as   D. insignificant to

II. Decide whether the following statements are TRUE, FALSE, or NOT GIVEN according to the information given in the text.

1. Marshall McLuhan is the first person to come up with the term "global village".

2. In the process of globalization, economies of different nations are becoming more and more independent.

   _____

3. Globalization to a great extent has internationalized the workforce, and has brought more opportunities than challenges to individuals and organizations.

   _____

4. The "either/or" binary thinking helps us expand the range of options when tackling intercultural problems.

   _____

5. Normally individualists are more likely to challenge themselves and develop hybrid identities than collectivists.

   _____

6. The development of ethnocentrism can be partly attributed to cultural socialization.

   _____

Checking Basic Concepts

Complete the following statements with a proper word or phrase in the box. Each word or phrase can be used only once.

| diversity | globalization | ethnicity | heterogeneity |
| ethnocentrism | identity | global village | self-awareness |

1. _____ is the belief that our own culture is the center of the universe, and that our way of doing things is better than others.

2. Your _____ is who you think you are and who others think you are.

3. Marshall McLuhan would remind us what occurs in one corner of the _____ will invariably affect other corners since it is now wired and connected.

Unit 1 Imperatives for Intercultural Communication

4. Now universities are more likely to argue that racial _____ is valuable for its own sake.

5. Unlike most countries in the world, we do not define citizenship based on race or _____.

6. _____ is the ongoing integration of the world economy.

7. Your _____ is your knowledge and understanding of your own character.

8. _____ means consisting of different or dissimilar elements.

Language in Use

I. Complete the following sentences with the words in the box. Change the form if necessary. Each word can be used only once.

| immigration | commitment | promote | negotiation | approach |
| acquire | forge | appealing | norm | emphasis |

1. Most students attend university mainly to _____ the knowledge needed for their chosen profession.

2. The government has a(n) _____ to provide urban citizens with improved community services and facilities.

3. Their outward appearance seems rather _____ because they come in a variety of styles, textures, and colors.

4. It is the lack of communication and _____ rather than frequent economic exchanges that results in the collisions (冲突) between different cultures.

5. The consensus among most economists is that _____, both legal and illegal, provides a small net boost to the economy.

6. The Prime Minister is determined to _____ a good relationship with America's new leader.

7. The singer has announced a full British tour to _____ his second solo album.

8. Non-smoking is now the _____ in most workplaces.

9. Employers are interested in how you _____ problems.

10. Placing too much _____ on being a good team player can negatively affect your career growth.

II. Paraphrase the following sentences from Text A.

1. One of the most important reasons for studying intercultural communication is to gain an awareness of one's own cultural identity and background.

   _____
   _____
   _____

2. As noted by writer Carol Hymowitz of *The Wall Street Journal*, "if companies are going to sell products and services globally, then they will need a rich mix of employees with varied perspectives and experiences. They will need top executives who understand different countries and cultures."

   _____
   _____
   _____

Expanding Intercultural Knowledge

How Is a Community Formed?

Do you know how the word "community" comes about and what messages it conveys? Look at the picture on the next page and tell how the word "community" is formed or which two words are combined together to possibly form the word "community". Then try to describe the defining characteristics of a community. Locate some of the words in the picture that you think are particularly important in forming a community and describe what they mean to the building of the community. Can you imagine what a community of a shared future is like?

Unit 1 Imperatives for Intercultural Communication

The concept of community may include two meanings: communication and unity. The two are related either in terms of causes and effects or in terms of means and ends. Communication is obviously the precondition of unity and community, or community is the ultimate goal of communication. Communication is culture and culture is communication. Without communication, there will be no unity, culture, or community, therefore, a community is in nature a communication community. Community is an integral part of the process of communication, and moreover, the ultimate goal. Inherent in and through the process of communication are the communicable values and ethics（道德规范） that form a particular community.

By extension, the building of a human life community, or a community of a shared future, is not only an integral part but the ultimate goal of intercultural communication. Intercultural communication creates favorable conditions for the possibility of a community of shared future. A community as such by nature is an intercultural communication community, or ideally an intercultural dialog community.

The term "communication" is also inherently related to the word "commonality", which suggests the idea that people communicate and live together on the commonly shared ground. Commonality shared by human beings in fact constitutes the foundation for a community of a shared future for mankind.

To prepare for a community of a shared future is the ideal fulfillment of intercultural communication. This is where the educational value, rather than the practical value of intercultural communication, lies. The implication is obvious: the building of a community of a shared future through intercultural communication is the ultimate goal of intercultural communication.

(Source: Jia Yuxin, *Experiencing Global Intercultural Communication*)

跨文化交际英语阅读教程
Intercultural Communication: An English Reading Coursebook

Reflecting and Discussing

1. Can you explain how a community is formed?
2. What do you think "a community of a shared future" is like? How can we build such a community?

Unit 1 Imperatives for Intercultural Communication

 Case Study

Discuss with your classmates the questions according to each case.

 Case 1

A Human Approach to World Peace

Today we are so interdependent, so closely interconnected with each other, that without a sense of universal responsibility, a feeling of universal brotherhood and sisterhood, and an understanding and belief that we really are part of one big human family, we cannot hope to overcome the dangers to our very existence—let alone bring about peace and happiness.

One nation's problems can no longer be satisfactorily solved by itself alone; too much depends on the interest, attitude, and cooperation of other nations. A universal humanitarian (人道主义) approach to world problems seems the only sound basis for world peace...

...The global population is increasing, and our resources are being rapidly depleted (大量减少). Look at the trees, for example. No one knows exactly what adverse effects massive deforestation will have on the climate, the soil, and global ecology as a whole. We are facing problems because people are concentrating only on their short-term, selfish interests, not thinking of the entire human family. They are not thinking of the earth and the long-term effects on universal life as a whole. If we of the present generation do not think about these now, future generations may not be able to cope with them.

(Source: Stella Ting-Toomey & Leeva C. Chung, *Understanding Intercultural Communication*)

1. Why does the author believe one nation's problems can no longer be satisfactorily solved by itself alone?

2. What "shared global concerns" do you think the international community faces?

Case 2

A Win-Win Cooperation

As a witness to China-Pakistan cooperation, Pakistani Prime Minister Shaukat Aziz made enthusiastic comments on the joint pursuit of the Belt and Road Initiative in an interview. He noted that he was very pleased to see this kind of Initiative in Pakistan, and that the government of Pakistan had taken many measures to implement it very seriously and effectively. Pakistan and China have a border linkage. People can drive to Pakistan and come back, and so it would be convenient to become involved in the Initiative. Pakistan, he noted, had also landed many other infrastructure (基础设施) projects which would be beneficial for the country and the people. The quality of people's life would be improved, as they would get jobs and achieve a better standard of living. Pakistan would borrow money from China to build these projects, and pay back after the projects have been built. So the Prime Minister believes this could be a good chance to establish a strong tie between Pakistan and China, which is beneficial for both countries. China has demonstrated to Pakistan what a dependable and reliable friend it can be. According to the Prime Minister, the China-Pakistan relationship is unique, particularly in the aspects of security cooperation and investments. The Initiative is clearly a win-win cooperation for both.

(Source: Hou Hongye, *Intercultural Reading: Appreciating Cultural Diversity*)

1. What attitude does Pakistani Prime Minister Shaukat Aziz show towards the Belt and Road Initiative?
2. What do you think the Belt and Road Initiative can bring to the world?

Unit 2 Communication and Culture

The greatest distance between people is not geographical space, but culture.

—Jamake Highwater

性相近,习相远。

——《三字经》

Learning Objectives

Upon completion of this unit, you will be able to:

- Understand the characteristics of communication and culture.
- Explain the relationship between communication and culture.
- Understand the meaning of intercultural communication.
- Define such terms as *communication*, *culture* and *intercultural communication*.
- Gain an insight into culture through analogies.
- Understand, interpret and critically evaluate different cultural behaviors.

Lead-in

A Monkey Exploring the Great World

Once upon a time, a monkey decided to leave the forest and explore the great, wide world. He traveled to the city and saw many strange and wonderful things but finally he decided to return home. Back in the forest his friends and relatives gathered around. "Well," they cried, "what did you see?"

"I saw buildings made of concrete and glass. Buildings so high that they touched the sky," said the monkey. And all his friends and relatives imagined glass branches scratching the sky. "The buildings were full of people walking on two legs and carrying briefcases," said the monkey. And his friends and relatives could almost see the people running along the branches with their tails wrapped firmly around their briefcases.

(Source: Jean Brick, *China: A Handbook in Intercultural Communication*)

Questions for Intercultural Understanding

1. Why did the monkeys imagine the scene "the people running along the branches with their tails wrapped around their briefcases"?
2. When you come into contact with other unfamiliar cultures, would you look at them in a similar way as those monkeys see the outside world?

Unit 2 Communication and Culture

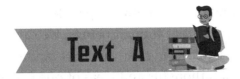

Communication and Culture: The Voice and the Echo

1   Culture and communication mutually influence one another, producing different behavioral **patterns** in different contexts. What, where and how we should talk are **regulated** by culture. Culture **shapes** our communication patterns, and communication in turn influences the structure of our culture. Indeed, the two are inseparable. In order to study intercultural communication, we must understand communication and culture and explore their relationship.

The Nature of Communication

2   Communication is everywhere. Every day, everywhere, people are communicating. Even when alone, people **are bombarded with** communication. Communication with others is the **essence** of what it means to be human. Through communication, people **conduct** their lives. People define themselves **via** their communication with others. *Communication* is the **vehicle** by which people **initiate**, maintain, and **terminate** their relationships with others. Communication is the means by which people influence and persuade others. Through communication, local, regional, national, and international conflicts are managed and resolved.

3   Although it constantly occurs around us, human communication is not at all a simple matter to define. Although there is no universally agreed-on definition of communication, most communication scholars agree on certain **dimensions** of communication that describe its nature.

4   Communication is a dynamic process. This means that communication is not a single event but an ongoing process, so that communicators are both senders and receivers of messages. When we are communicating, we are creating, maintaining or sharing meanings, which **implies** that people are actively involved in the communication process.

5   Communication is symbolic. A symbol is an expression that represents something else. Human beings use a symbol—be it a word, a sound, a mark on paper, a body movement or a painting—to pass on an idea or a feeling, or to seek information. The main reason communication is symbolic is that there is

no direct mind-to-mind contact between people. We cannot access the internal thoughts and feelings of other human beings; we can only **infer** what they are experiencing by what we see and hear. Symbols can be verbal or nonverbal. They are the vehicle by which thoughts and ideas of one person can be communicated to another.

6   Communication is contextual. Context refers to the cultural, physical, social and relational environment in which communication occurs. In many ways, context helps determine the words and actions we **generate** and the meanings we give to the symbols produced by other people. Reflect for a moment on how differently you would behave in each of the following settings: a classroom, a church, a funeral, a wedding, a sporting event or a nightclub. The simple phrase, "How are you?" **shifts** meaning as we move from place to place and person to person. To a friend, it serves as a friendly greeting. Yet in a doctor's office, the same three words asked by a doctor call for a detailed response.

7   Communication has a consequence. We are changing other people each time we exchange messages with them. What we say and do affects others: how they perceive themselves, how they think about themselves, and how they think about others. We in turn, are also changed by others in the interaction.

The Nature of Culture

8   Moving from communication to culture provides us with a rather **seamless** transition, for as American **anthropologist** Edward T. Hall[1] points out, "Culture is communication and communication is culture." In fact, when examining communication and culture, it is hard to decide which is the voice and which is the echo. The reason for the **duality** is that you learn your culture via communication, while at the same time communication is a reflection of your culture.

9   Like communication, *culture* is **ubiquitous** and **has a profound effect on** humans. While there are many explanations of what culture is and does, there is a general agreement on what **constitutes** its major characteristics. An examination of these characteristics will provide an increased understanding of this **abstract**, **multifaceted** concept and also **offer insight into** how communication is influenced by culture.

10   Culture is learned. At birth, we have no knowledge of the many societal rules needed to function effectively in our culture, but we quickly begin to **internalize** this information. Through interactions, observations, and **imitation**, the proper

ways of thinking, feeling, and behaving are communicated to us. Being taught to eat with a fork, a pair of chopsticks, or even one's fingers is learning cultural behavior. Attending a Catholic (天主教) Mass[2] on Sunday or praying at a Jewish the Synagogue (犹太教会堂) on Saturday is learning cultural behavior and values. Celebrating the Spring Festival, Christmas, or Ramadan[3] is learning cultural traditions. Culture is also acquired from art, **proverbs**, **folklore**, history, religion, and a variety of other sources. This learning, often referred to as **enculturation**, is both conscious and subconscious and has the objective of teaching the individual how to function properly within a specific cultural environment.

11   Culture is transmitted from generation to generation. You learn your culture from family members, teachers, peers, books, personal observations, and a host of media sources. The appropriate way to act, what to say, and things to value are all communicated to the members of your generation by these many sources. You are also a source for passing these cultural expectations to **succeeding** generations, usually with little or no variation. Culture represents our link to the past and, through future generations, hope for the future.

12   Culture is symbolic. Words, gestures, and images are merely symbols used to **convey** meaning. It is the ability to use these symbols that allows us to engage in the many forms of social **intercourse** used to construct and convey culture. Our symbol-making ability **facilitates** learning and enables transmission of meaning from one person to another, group to group, and generation to generation. In addition to transmission, the **portability** of symbols creates the ability to store information, which allows cultures to preserve what is considered important, and to create a history. The preservation of culture provides each new generation with a road map to follow and a reference library to consult when unknown situations are encountered. Succeeding generations may **modify** established behavior or values, or construct new ones, but the **accumulation** of past traditions is what we know as culture.

13   Culture is dynamic. Cultures are constantly changing over time. While some cultures readily embrace change, others tend to resist it. Within a culture, the introduction of new ideas, inventions, and exposure to other cultures contribute to transformation. Chinese culture, with its long history, has undergone significant changes, particularly since the May 4th Movement in 1919. Today, the changes in China are even more apparent and prominent, driven by the increasingly frequent contact with other countries. The very nature of contact brings about changes, and China's growing global engagement demonstrates this ongoing transformation.

14   Culture is ethnocentric. The strong sense of group identity, or **attachment**, produced by culture can lead to ethnocentrism, the tendency to view one's own culture as superior to others. Ethnocentrism can arise from enculturation. Being continually told that you live in the greatest country in the world or that your way of life is better than those of other nations, or your values are superior to those of other ethnic groups can lead to feelings of cultural superiority. Ethnocentrism can also result from a lack of contact with other cultures. If exposed only to one cultural orientation, it is likely that you would develop the idea that your way of life was superior, and you would tend to view the rest of the world from that perspective.

15   An inability to understand or accept different ways and customs can also **provoke** feelings of ethnocentrism. It is quite natural to feel at ease with people who are like you and **adhere to** the same social norms and **protocols**. It is usually easy to communicate when you know what to expect. It is also normal to feel uneasy when **confronted with** new and different social values, beliefs, and behavior. Communication is probably difficult when you do not know what to expect.

Intercultural Communication

16   Once we understand the meanings of communication and culture, it becomes clear that *intercultural communication* refers to the communication among people from two or more cultures. However, because we **are destined to** carry our cultural baggage whenever and wherever we go, when people are from two different cultures, communication is often more **complicated**. The potential for miscommunication and disagreement is greater because of cultural differences. Thus, the study of intercultural communication aims to understand the influence of culture on our attitudes, beliefs, and behavior in order to reduce misunderstandings that result from cultural variations.

(Source: Larry A. Samovar et al., *Communication Between Cultures*, Chapter 2 and Larry A. Samovar et al., *Intercultural Communication: A Reader*, Chapter 1)

 New Words

abstract   adj.   based on general ideas and not on any particular real person, thing, or situation 抽象的（与个别情况相对）；纯理论的

Unit 2 Communication and Culture

accumulation	n.	the acquisition or gradual gathering of sth. 积累，积聚，堆积
anthropologist	n.	a person who studies anthropology 人类学家
attachment	n.	belief in and support for an idea or a set of values 信念，信仰；忠诚；拥护
complicated	adj.	made of many different things or parts that are connected; difficult to understand 复杂的，难懂的
conduct	v.	to organize and/or do a particular activity 组织，安排，实施
constitute	v.	to be the parts that together form sth. 组成，构成
convey	v.	to make ideas, feelings, etc. known to sb. 表达，传递（思想、感情等）
dimension	n.	an aspect, or way of looking at or thinking about sth. 方面；侧面
duality	n.	the state of having two parts or aspects 双重性，二元性
enculturation	n.	the gradual acquisition of the characteristics and norms of a culture or group by a person, another culture, etc. 社会文化适应
essence	n.	the most important quality or feature of sth., that makes it what it is 本质，实质，精髓
facilitate	v.	to make an action or a process possible or easier 促进；使便利
folklore	n.	the traditional stories, customs, and habits of a particular community or nation 民间传说，民俗
generate	v.	to produce or create sth. 产生，引起
imitation	n.	the act of copying sb./sth. 模仿，仿效
imply	v.	to suggest that sth. is true or that you feel or think sth., without saying so directly 含有……的意思，暗示，暗指

infer	v.	to reach an opinion or decide that sth. is true on the basis of information that is available 推断，推论，推理
initiate	v.	to make sth. begin 开始，发起，创始
intercourse	n.	communication between people, countries, etc. 交往，交际
internalize	v.	to make a feeling, an attitude, or a belief part of the way you think and behave 使（感情、态度或信仰）成为思想行为的一部分，使内在化
modify	v.	to change sth. slightly, especially in order to make it more suitable for a particular purpose 调整，稍作修改；使更适合
multifaceted	adj.	having many different aspects to be considered 多方面的；要从多方面考虑的
pattern	n.	the regular way in which sth. happens or is done 模式，方式
portability	n.	the quality or state of being portable 轻便；可携带性
prominent	adj.	easily seen 显眼的，显著的，突出的
protocol	n.	a system of fixed rules and formal behavior used at official meetings, usually between governments 礼仪，外交礼节
proverb	n.	a short sentence that people often quote, because it gives advice or tells you sth. about life 谚语
provoke	v.	to cause a particular reaction or have a particular effect 激起，引起，引发
regulate	v.	to control sth. by means of rules（用规则条约）约束，控制
seamless	adj.	with no spaces or pauses between one part and the next 无间隙的
shape	v.	to have an important influence on the way that sb./sth. develops 决定……的形成，影响……的发展

Unit 2 Communication and Culture

shift	v.	to change from one state, position, etc. to another 变换，更替
succeeding	adj.	following, after 随后的，接着的
terminate	v.	to end; to make sth. end（使）停止，结束，终止
ubiquitous	adj.	seeming to be everywhere or in several places at the same time; very common 似乎无所不在的，十分普遍的
vehicle	n.	sth. that can be used to express your ideas or feelings or as a way of achieving sth.（赖以表达思想、感情或达到目的的）手段，工具
via	prep.	by means of a particular person, system, etc. 通过，凭借（某人、系统等）

Useful Expressions

adhere to	to behave according to a particular law, rule, set of instructions, etc.; to follow a particular set of beliefs or a fixed way of doing sth. 坚持，遵守，遵循（法律、规章、指示、信念等）
be bombarded with	to be repeatedly suject to sth., usually in a rapid or overwhelming manner 被……（大量地）轰炸，被……淹没
be confronted with	to be faced with; to be up against 面临，面对
be destined to	to be bound to 注定
have a profound effect on	to strongly affect 对……有着深远的影响
offer insight into sth.	to give an understanding of what sth. is like 深刻理解，洞察

Cultural Notes

1. Edward T. Hall

Edward Twitchell Hall, Jr. (1914–2009) was an American anthropologist and cross-cultural researcher, the first person to systematically study cross-cultural communication activities.

He is the author of the books *The Silent Language* (1959) and *Beyond Culture* (1976), the foundation work of intercultural communication. He is regarded as the founding father of intercultural communication due to his great contribution to this field.

2. Mass

Mass is a Christian church ceremony, especially in a Roman Catholic, during which people eat bread and drink wine in order to remember the last meal of Jesus Christ.

3. Ramadan

Ramadan (also spelled "Ramazan" "Ramzan" "Ramadhan" or "Ramathan") is the ninth month of the Islamic calendar（伊斯兰历法）, observed by Muslims worldwide as a month of fasting（斋戒）, prayer, reflection and community. Ramadan lasts 29–30 days, from one sighting of the crescent moon（新月）to the next. The spiritual rewards of fasting are believed to be multiplied during Ramadan. Accordingly, during the hours of fasting, Muslims refrain not only from food and drink, but also from tobacco products, sexual relations, and sinful behaviors, devoting themselves instead to prayer and study of the Quran（古兰经）.

Reading Comprehension

I. Choose the best options to answer the following questions or fill in the blanks.

1. What's mainly discussed in the text?
   A. The nature of communication.
   B. The nature of culture.
   C. The interrelationship between communication and culture.
   D. All the above.

2. How does the text describe communication as a process?
   A. A static event.
   B. A one-time occurrence.
   C. An ongoing and dynamic process.
   D. A passive transmission of information.

3. What is the main reason for communication being symbolic according to the text?
   A. To create confusion.
   B. To allow direct mind-to-mind contact.
   C. To facilitate access to internal thoughts.
   D. Due to the absence of mind-to-mind contact.

Unit 2 Communication and Culture

4. The fact that a simple phrase like "How are you?" might shift meaning in different settings is used to exemplify that _____.

    A. communication is dynamic

    B. communication is symbolic

    C. communication is contextual

    D. communication has a consequence

5. According to the text, which of the following is NOT a characteristic of "culture"?

    A. Culture is contextual.

    B. Culture is learned.

    C. Culture is transmitted from generation to generation.

    D. Culture is dynamic and symbolic.

6. Which of the following is NOT true about the statement "Culture is learned" in Paragraph 10?

    A. Humans are born with the knowledge of the social norms in their culture.

    B. Culture can be acquired through art, folklore and religion.

    C. Cultural behavior can be learned through interactions, observations and imitation in daily communication.

    D. The learning process can be either conscious or subconscious.

7. According to the author, what's NOT true about "ethnocentrism" in Paragraph 14?

    A. A strong sense of one's own cultural identity might lead to ethnocentrism.

    B. Ethnocentrism refers to a tendency to view one's own culture as superior to others.

    C. Ethnocentrism can result from close contact with other cultures.

    D. An inability to understand or accept different ways and customs can give rise to ethnocentrism.

II. **Decide whether the following statements are TRUE, FALSE, or NOT GIVEN according to the information given in the text.**

1. The "voice-echo" metaphor is an indication of the inseparable relationship between communication and culture, the former of which is the voice, while the latter is the echo.

31

2. There is a general agreement on the definition of "communication".

3. Human beings use more verbal than nonverbal messages to transfer meanings.

4. Context may help us generate particular words and actions, and assign specific meanings to the symbols produced by others in the course of communication.

5. Symbols are important when they facilitate the transmission of meanings in communication and make the preservation of culture possible.

6. If one is exposed and confined only to one culture, it's more likely for him/her to feel uneasy when confronted with different social values, beliefs and behavior.

7. Miscommunication and disagreement are more likely to occur when there are more cultural differences or variations.

Checking Basic Concepts

Complete the following statements with a proper word or phrase in the box. Each word or phrase can be used only once.

| communication | context | culture | enculturation |
| dynamic | symbol | intercultural communication | |

1. _____ refers to the physical or social situation in which communication occurs.

Unit 2 Communication and Culture

2. _____ can be defined as the learned patterns of behavior and attitudes shared by a group of people.

3. The process in which you learn your own cultural behavior, traditions and values from family members, teachers, peers, books, personal observations, and a host of media sources is called _____.

4. _____ is the interaction between people from different cultural backgrounds.

5. Kungfu and Panda are regarded as two _____ of Chinese culture.

6. _____ is a symbolic process whereby meaning is shared and negotiated.

7. Communication is _____, because it is active and always changing.

Language in Use

I. **Complete the following sentences with the words in the box. Change the form if necessary. Each word can be used only once.**

facilitate	constitute	initiate	imply	accumulation
shape	terminate	insight	modify	provoke

1. Fundamentally, intelligence is a(n) _____ of skills—not an innate thing.

2. The government has to _____ a program of economic reform to tackle the current slowdown of the economy.

3. One's education is bound to _____ his worldview.

4. China's ethnic minority _____ less than seven percent of its total population.

5. A dispute occurring in the communication would probably abruptly _____ the trade.

6. The results of the survey _____ more people are aware of the significance of protecting cultural diversity.

7. The study of language acquisition, to a large extent, offers direct _____ into how humans learn.

8. We should learn to grasp communication skills, for they can _____ mutual understanding.

9. The article was intended to _____ discussion on the imperative of intercultural communication among the public.

10. Patients are taught how to _____ their diet.

II. Paraphrase the following sentences from Text A.

1. When we are communicating, we are creating, maintaining or sharing meanings, which implies that people are actively involved in the communication process.

   _____
   _____
   _____

2. Our symbol-making ability facilitates learning and enables transmission of meaning from one person to another, group to group, and generation to generation.

   _____
   _____
   _____

Expanding Intercultural Knowledge

Chinese Translation of "Communication"

Owing to its complexity, the term "communication" does not have a single equivalent in Chinese. Many terms have been used to translate "communication". They are "交际""交流""传播""沟通""通信". In the Chinese mainland, each of these terms is preferred by a certain discipline:

- 交际 in the field of linguistics
- 交流 in the field of psychology
- 传播 in the field of journalism

Unit 2 Communication and Culture

- 沟通 in the field of management
- 通信 in the field of communication

Cultural Analogy

An analogy is a comparison of one thing with another thing that has similar features. Because the term "culture" is too complex and abstract to define, analogies between culture and concrete and vivid things or images in our lives can help us better understand what culture is and how it operates to make us human beings as cultural and social beings.

Culture is like an iceberg

Just as an iceberg has parts that are visible on the water surface and parts that are not visible below the water surface, culture is also divided into visible and invisible parts.

The culture on the water surface includes people's behaviors, food, clothing, language, visual arts, festivals, etc. These are visible and easy to find.

Underwater culture includes concepts, notions, values, views, judgements, beliefs, attitudes towards different things, etc. These parts account for much more than the visible culture, and they are more difficult to discover and learn.

Culture is our software

Culture is the basic operating system that makes us human. Humans around the world are physically pretty much the same. There are variations in body size, shape and color, but the basic equipment is universal. We can think of our physical selves as the hardware, but the hardware does not work without software. It is the culture that provides us with the needed software, however, as with any good software, we are only vaguely aware of it when we use it.

Culture is like the water a fish swims in

A fish notices everything around it except the water in which it is swimming. The fish just takes the water for granted as it is always there around it. The same is true for us. Our culture is so much a part of who we are and what the world is like for us that we do not notice it. We take it for granted.

Culture is like an onion

Culture is like an onion, a system that can be peeled, layer by layer, in order to reveal the content. Specifically, culture is made of three layers around a core.

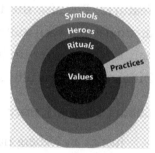

(Source: Hofstede G. & Hofstede G. J., 2005)

The first skin of the onion is "symbols", which is the easiest to perceive by an outsider. Words, gestures, pictures, hairstyles, or flags, etc., belong to this category. The second skin is "heroes", referring to the kind of people worshiped in a culture. Batman in the United States and Money King in China can serve as cultural heroes respectively. The third layer is "rituals", the collective activities that are considered socially essential within a culture. Wedding ceremonies and funerals, for instance, are rituals. In the center of the onion are the core of a culture—values, a set of rules that underlie people's behavior. Values are the deepest manifestation of a culture.

Symbols, heroes and rituals, the three outer layers of the onion, have been included in the category of practices referring to what people do. They are visible and obvious to an outside observer. Values, by determining practices, can indicate why people do what they do. They are the most difficult to be understood by an outsider.

Culture is the grammar of our behavior

Culture is what people need to know in order to behave appropriately in any society. It includes all the rules that make actions meaningful to those acting and to the people around them.

(Source: Linell Davis, *Doing Culture: Cross-Cultural Communication in Action*)

Unit 2 Communication and Culture

Reflecting and Discussing

1. Which of the analogies mentioned in the text do you like best? Why?
2. Can you use another analogy to describe or explain your own understanding of what culture is and does. You can use the following format to create your own analogy:

   Culture is _____ or is like _____, because _____.

Text B Questions of Culture

Read Text B and do the exercises online.

Case Study

Discuss with your classmates the questions according to each case.

Case 1

A Fish in Unfamiliar Waters

A Chinese student, confident in her knowledge of American culture, prepares to give a speech in English appropriate for an international audience for an English-speaking contest. In the speech, she paraphrases Martin Luther King by using the phrase "I have a dream". She is confident that her intended international audience will understand the reference.

She is right. The audience will know that she is quoting Martin Luther King, but they won't necessarily be impressed. King's speech was given more than 50 years ago and is so widely known that quoting it may be considered too simple, as saying what has already been said too many times. To most Americans and many other Westerners, time flies by very quickly, so using an out-of-date metaphor (比喻) reveals you to be out of date.

In Chinese culture, a writer or speaker shows his/her learning by quoting famous people from the past. It is not necessary to say where the quote comes from. The audience will know and respect your knowledge. In the United States, people rarely quote famous people from the past unless it is an especially sentimental or patriotic (爱国的) occasion where it is understood that old and familiar images should be remembered.

Americans like to do something unexpectedly. An advertising executive may get his/her audience's attention by quoting the ancient Greek philosopher Plato (柏拉图), while a university professor might cleverly surprise an academic audience by using the famous Nike advertisement when he/she says, "Just do it."

If you quote Martin Luther King, some listeners may suspect you of mocking (嘲笑) them, as it is considered clever to quote a famous saying in an ironic (反讽的) or satirical (讽刺的) way.

(Source: Linell Davis, *Doing Culture: Cross-Cultural Communication in Action*)

Unit 2 Communication and Culture

1. Why does the Chinese student quote Martin Luther King in her speech?

2. Is it appropriate to quote Martin Luther King for her international audience? Why or why not?

3. Do you have any suggestions for her if she wants to impress her international audience?

 Case 2

How Long Is Your Mum Going to Stay?

Read the story told by Litz, a Finn, who married a Chinese doctor.

My husband and I had long wished to bring his mother to stay with us for a while. Last summer, after we redecorated our house, we invited her over. You can well imagine how happy my husband was! And I was just as happy. I know being filial (孝顺的) to parents is a great value Chinese people cherish. As the wife of a Chinese man, I try to be as filial as my husband.

Two days after my mother-in-law's arrival, I talked to my husband while his mother was sitting in the garden enjoying the sunshine.

Litz: Dick, how long is your mum going to stay?

Dick: I don't know. I haven't asked her.

Litz: Why not ask her?

Dick: What do you mean by asking her?

Litz: I mean what I said. Just ask her how long she is going to stay.

My mother-in-law overheard our conversation, and decided to leave for China that very afternoon. I had never expected that her visit would be so short. I tried very hard to persuade her to change her mind, but in vain.

(Source: Wang Rong & Zhang Ailin, *Bridge Between Minds: Intercultural Communication*)

1. Why did the mother-in-law insist on leaving after she overheard the conversation between her son and daughter-in-law?

2. What did Litz really mean when she asked how long her mother-in-law was going to stay?

3. Have you ever experienced any misunderstandings while communicating with people from different cultural backgrounds? If yes, describe your experience, and explain the reasons for the misunderstanding.

Unit 3
Perception and Culture

Perception is reality. It's not what you say, but what is heard. It's not what you show, but what is seen. It's not what you mean, but what is understood.

—*Prany Sananikone*

甲之蜜糖，乙之砒霜。

——亦舒

Learning Objectives

Upon completion of this unit, you will be able to:

- Understand the nature and the process of human perception.
- Understand how culture influences perception.
- Define such terms as *perception*, *selection*, *categorization* and *interpretation*.
- Know the perceived meanings of colors and animals in Chinese and Western cultures.
- Increase your understanding of how China is perceived by Western countries and the reasons behind the perception.
- Understand, interpret and critically evaluate different cultural behaviors.

Lead-in

Gift

Mark is a Canadian who is currently working in China. When he had just started his work in China, a Chinese couple invited him to their newly-decorated house as a sign of hospitality. Mark bought a very new exquisite (精美的) clock which he thought would go well with their house. However, the couple looked very offended and refused to take his gift.

(Source: Huang Yucai, *A New Comparison of English and Chinese Languages and Cultures*)

Questions for Intercultural Understanding

1. What do you think caused the embarrassing situation?
2. What should Mark have done?

Unit 3 Perception and Culture

Becoming a Sensitive Intercultural Perceiver

1   An Asian American professor used to observe his American students' reactions when he told them that people in some Asian countries eat pig ears, chicken feet, fish **innards**, and the meat of dogs and snakes. As expected, the most common reaction was, "Yuck! It's **disgusting**," accompanied by a look of **stunned** disbelief on their faces. Why do the students feel this way, and what makes them produce this kind of reaction? This article will answer these questions by examining human perception and how our perception depends on our cultural experiences.

Perception Defined

2   Human *perception* is an active process by which we use our sensory organs to sense the world. Using our nervous system and brains, the process allows us to recognize and identify the existence of all kinds of **stimuli** and then **evaluate** and **interpret** what we identify. In other words, *perception* is a process by which we make what we sense into a meaningful experience by selecting, **categorizing**, and interpreting internal and external stimuli to form our view of the world. Internal stimuli include our nervous system, desires, interests, and motivations. External stimuli are the sensations that come from the way we see, smell, touch, hear and taste.

Stages of the Perception Process

3   The process of perception **is** thus **composed of** three stages: selection, categorization, and interpretation. Each of these steps is affected by culture.

4   *Selection* is the first step. It is the major part of the perception process of **converting** the environmental stimuli into a meaningful experience. As we face a large variety of stimuli every day, we **are** only **capable of** perceiving part of them through a selective process. For example, in an interesting study (as shown in the picture on the next page), participants viewed a videotape of a basketball game. They were told to count the number of passes one team made. In the video, a woman dressed up as a gorilla walks into the game, turns to face the camera, and beats her fists on her chest. Fifty percent of all the people who watched the video failed to notice the gorilla. This study indicates people may fail to perceive any object unless they are paying direct, focused attention to that object. When we

need something, or have an interest in it, we are more likely to sense it out of competing stimuli. For example, when we're hungry, we're more likely to **attend to** food advertisements.

(Source: Selective Attention Test by Simons & Chabris, 1999)

5   Being in a busy airport **terminal** is another example. While there, we are confronted with many competing stimuli. We simply cannot attend to everything. However, if an announcement is made asking us by name to report to the ticket **counter**, we would probably hear our name even in that noisy environment.

6   The second step in the perception process is *categorization*. Along with selecting stimuli from the environment, we must organize them in some meaningful way. When we observe a building, our attention is not directed towards the thousands of individual pieces; instead, we focus on the unified whole of the building. Similarly, when people are asked to define a human being, some may describe it based on skin color, while others may consider it from the perspective of race or nationality.

7   Culture plays an essential part in organizing the environment. In one **illustrative** study, children from China and the United States were presented with pictures that **consisted of** three objects (e.g. a man, a woman and a baby) and were asked to pick two objects out of the three that went together. In this case, which two objects would you place together? The man and the woman? The woman and the baby? Or the man and the baby?

8   Whereas American children tended to group objects based on shared **analytic** features or shared categories, that is, the same categorization term could

be applied to both (e.g. The man and the woman were grouped together because "they are both adults".), Chinese children preferred to group objects on the basis of relationship (e.g. The woman and the baby were grouped together because "the mother takes care of the baby".). Other researchers **replicated** the findings with Chinese and American college students. The results **indicate** that culture influences our perceptual categorization.

9   The third step in the perception process is *interpretation*. When we select and categorize the external stimuli into stable groups or patterns, we try to make sense of the groups or patterns by assigning meaning to them. The same situation can be interpreted quite differently by diverse people. A police officer arriving at a crime scene can be perceived by the **victim** as calming and **relief** giving but as **fearsome** and threatening by the **criminal**.

10   The interpretation process plays a very important role in intercultural interaction. For example, an American audience may interpret the smiles on the faces of Japanese athletes after being terribly defeated by their **opponents** as indicating that Japanese athletes don't care about their losing the game. However, from the Japanese perspective, the same smile is interpreted as a painful expression that is used to cover the embarrassment of being defeated. A kiss in public may just represent a way of saying hello in the West, but is viewed as "love-making" in Sri Lanka (斯里兰卡).

11   It is important to note that although we treat the three stages of perception separately, in reality, they are an **integrated** process with no **clear-cut boundaries** between them.

Cultural Influence on Perception

12   As mentioned previously, a person's culture has a strong impact on the perception process. Culture not only provides the foundation for the meanings we give to our perceptions, but it also directs us to interpret specific kinds of messages and events. For example, the moon is a rocky **sphere** that orbits the earth; yet when looking at this object, many Americans often see a man in the moon, many Native Americans perceive a rabbit, whereas Chinese claim a lady is **fleeing** her husband. For Americans, a "V" sign made with two fingers usually represents victory, but Australians **equate** this gesture **with** a rude American gesture usually made with the middle finger. While most Asians respond negatively to white flowers because white **is associated with** death, for Peruvians (秘鲁人), Iranians (伊朗人), and Mexicans, yellow flowers instead often **invoke**

the same reaction.

13   In these three examples, the external objects (moon, gesture and flowers) are the same, yet people's responses to them are different across cultures. The reason is perception and cultural **symbolism**. Comprehending how a person's perception is affected by his/her culture is helpful in understanding not only one's own behavior but also the behavior of others. The more you understand how your own cultural values and experiences influence your perceptions and how others may look at behavior from their own cultural lens, the more likely you are to engage in competent intercultural communication.

(Source: Guo-Ming Chen & Willian J. Starosta, *Foundations of Intercultural Communication,* Chapter 3)

New Words

analytic	*adj.*	using a logical method of thinking about sth. in order to understand it, especially by looking at all the parts separately 分析的，解析的，分析性的
boundary	*n.*	a real or imagined line that marks the limits or edges of sth. and separates it from other things or places; a dividing line 边界；界限
categorize	*v.*	to put people or things into groups according to what type they are 将……分类，把……加以归类
clear-cut	*adj.*	definite and easy to see or identify 明确的，明显的，易辨认的
convert	*v.*	to change or make sth. change from one form, purpose, system, etc. to another（使）转变，转换，转化
counter	*n.*	a long flat surface over which goods are sold or business is done in a shop/store, bank, etc.（商店、银行等的）柜台
criminal	*n.*	a person who commits a crime 罪犯
disgusting	*adj.*	extremely unpleasant and making you feel slightly ill 令人不快的，使人厌恶的，令人恶心的，使人作呕的
evaluate	*v.*	to form an opinion of the amount, value or quality of sth. after thinking about it carefully 估计，评价，评估

Unit 3 Perception and Culture

fearsome	*adj.*	making people feel very frightened 很可怕的，十分吓人的
flee	*v.*	to leave a person or place very quickly, especially because you are afraid of possible danger 迅速离开，（尤指害怕有危险而）逃跑
illustrative	*adj.*	helping to explain sth. or show it more clearly with examples or pictures 解释性的；图解的
indicate	*v.*	to show that sth. is true or exists 表明，显示
innards	*n.*	(*pl.*) the organs inside the body of a person or an animal, especially the stomach 内脏；（尤指）胃
integrated	*adj.*	with two or more things combined in order to become more effective 各部分密切协调的，综合的，完整统一的
interpret	*v.*	to decide that sth. has a particular meaning and to understand it in this way 把……理解为，领会
invoke	*v.*	to make sb. have a particular feeling or imagine a particular scene 使产生，唤起，引起（感情或想象）
opponent	*n.*	a person that you are playing or fighting against in a game, competition, argument, etc. 对手，竞争者
relief	*n.*	the feeling of happiness that you have when sth. unpleasant stops or does not happen（不快过后的）宽慰，轻松；解脱
replicate	*v.*	to do someone's experiment, work, or research yourself in exactly the same way 复制，重做（试验、工作或研究）
sphere	*n.*	any object that is completely round, for example, a ball 圆球；球状物
stimuli	*n.*	(*pl.* of stimulus) things that encourage activity in people or things 刺激物
stunned	*adj.*	extremely shocked or surprised by sth. and therefore unable to speak or do anything 震惊的
symbolism	*n.*	the use of symbols to represent ideas, especially in art and literature（尤指文艺中的）象征主义，象征手法
terminal	*n.*	a building or set of buildings at an airport where air passengers arrive and leave 航站楼，航空终点站

| victim | n. | a person who has been attacked, injured, or killed as the result of a crime, a disease, an accident, etc. 受害者，罹难者 |

Useful Expressions

attend to	to pay attention to what sb. is saying or doing 注意，专心
be associated with	to have a connection or correlation with sth. 有关联的，相关的
be capable of	to have the ability or qualities necessary for doing sth. 有能力做……；能够
be composed of	to be formed as a whole by combining different things together 由……组成
consist of	to be made of or formed from sth. 以……为组成部分
equate with	to think that sth. is the same as sth. else or is as important 同等看待；使等同

Reading Comprehension

I. Choose the best options to answer the following questions or fill in the blanks.

1. What is the text mainly about?
   A. An in-depth exploration of the diversity of cultures.
   B. A research on different reactions towards culture.
   C. An exploration of human perception and how it is influenced by cultural experiences.
   D. A research on the three stages of perception process.

2. According to Paragraph 2, which of the following statements about "stimuli" is **NOT** true?
   A. Stimuli can be identified by our nervous system and brains.
   B. Stimuli can be both internal and external.
   C. Human perception can be realized through an active process of selecting, organizing and interpreting all kinds of stimuli.

D. Human desires and motivations are good examples of external stimuli.

3. The process of perception consists of the following stages **EXCEPT**_____.
   A. selection   B. attention
   C. categorization   D. interpretation

4. According to Paragraph 4, in the videotape of a basketball game, the woman dressed as a gorilla failed to draw the attention of half of the audience mainly because _____.
   A. the woman who dressed herself as a gorilla was not so attractive
   B. the audience couldn't focus in the environment of competing stimuli
   C. the audience were only capable of perceiving part of the stimuli through a selective process
   D. the audience were incapable of converting the environment stimuli into meaningful experiences

5. Which of the following examples from the text **BEST** illustrates the statement?
   "Culture plays an essential part in organizing the environment." (Paragraph 7)
   A. Being in a busy airport terminal, one can catch his or her name effortlessly in the announcement.
   B. American children tend to group a man and a woman together, whereas Chinese children tend to group a woman and a baby together.
   C. A policeman at the crime scene can be viewed as calming and relief giving by the victims, but as fearsome and threatening by the criminals.
   D. A kiss in public may be a way of greeting in the West, but is viewed as "lovemaking" in Sri Lanka.

6. Which of the following statements about the Japanese athletes' smiles is most likely to be true?
   A. The American audience may interpret the smiles as a painful expression covering their embarrassment of being defeated.
   B. The Japanese may think that they do not care about their losing of the game.
   C. The interpretation of the smile is conditioned by one's culture.
   D. The interpretation of the smile varies from person to person as our cognitive ability to perceive the world might be different.

7. According to the text, a person's _____ has a huge impact on the perception process.
   A. cultural background
   B. physical appearance
   C. individual personality
   D. language competence

II. Decide whether the following statements are TRUE, FALSE, or NOT GIVEN according to the information given in the text.

1. Human perception refers to an active process by which humans use sensory organs to sense the world.

   _____

2. While American college students tend to group objects based on shared analytic features, Chinese college students prefer to group objects on the basis of relationship.

   _____

3. There are obvious boundaries between different stages of human perceptual process.

   _____

4. White flowers can arouse negative reactions from Asians, Peruvians, as well as Mexicans.

   _____

5. A good comprehension of how a person's perception is affected by his or her culture is inseparable from one's cognitive ability.

   _____

6. The more one understands the roles that culture plays in human perception, the more likely he or she could engage in effective intercultural communication.

   _____

Unit 3 Perception and Culture

Checking Basic Concepts

Complete the following statements with a proper word or phrase in the box. Each word or phrase can be used only once.

> categorization   cultural lens   interpretation   perception   selection

1. _____ is the process by which we select, organize, and interpret external and internal stimuli to create our view of the world.

2. While scanning a newspaper, different people may pay attention to different information: young people may focus on entertainment, sports and movie issues, and politicians may be interested in political news, while housewives may show interest in items for daily use. This process of perception is called _____.

3. _____ refers to arranging or organizing information into meaningful groups or patterns.

4. _____ is the process in which people try to make sense of their physical and social world by attaching meaning to them.

5. A(n) _____ is another term for viewing things from the perspective of a foreign culture.

Language in Use

I. **Complete the following sentences with the words in the box. Change the form if necessary. Each word can be used only once.**

> indicate   evaluate   convert   equate   associate
> relief   consist   interpret   opponent   replicate

1. Their diet _____ largely of vegetables.

2. Students are asked to _____ their professors' quality of teaching at the end of the semester.

3. The fascination of the game lies in trying to guess what the _____ is thinking.

4. We can develop our analytical skills and learn how to view and _____ the

world around us in different ways.

5. Although his experiment achieved a number of groundbreaking findings, the subsequent experiments failed to _____ these findings.

6. The hotel is going to be _____ into a nursing home.

7. The bar charts (柱状图) _____ children's cultural awareness is positively related with their levels of education.

8. For a majority of freshmen, it is a(n) _____ to be able to talk about the issues in both their studies and lives to a consultant.

9. Chinese people tend to _____ the color "white" with "death".

10. Some parents _____ education with exam success.

II. Paraphrase the following sentences from Text A.

1. Perception is a process by which we make what we sense into a meaningful experience by selecting, categorizing, and interpreting internal and external stimuli to form our view of world.

   _____
   _____
   _____

2. Comprehending how a person's perception is affected by his or her culture is helpful in understanding not only one's own behavior but also the behavior of others.

   _____
   _____
   _____

Expanding Intercultural Knowledge

Symbolic Meanings of Colors in Different Cultures

Colors may have different symbolic meanings across cultures, so people from different cultural backgrounds would assign a totally different set of meanings to each color.

Unit 3 Perception and Culture

- Red represents longevity, splendor, and wealth to Chinese, Japanese, and Koreans, and it is a wedding color in parts of India.
- Black is very much welcome in the Caribbean (加勒比地区) and Africa.
- Green is a holy color to Moslems (穆斯林教徒).
- Yellow is a noble color for Chinese and Indians.
- White is a wedding color in the United States, but a funeral color in India.

The following is the perceived meaning of different colors by Americans.

Color	Symbolic meaning
black	death, evil, mourning, sexy
blue	cold, masculine, sad, sky
green	envy, greed, money
pink	feminine, shy, softness, sweet
red	anger, hot, love, sex
white	good, innocent, peaceful, pure
yellow	caution, happy, sunshine, warm

(Source: Guo-Ming Chen & Willian J. Starosta, *Foundations of Intercultural Communication*)

Reflecting and Discussing

I. Work in groups. Each group does a survey of the symbolic meanings of the colors listed in the table in one country (China, Japan, India, Britain, France, Russia, Brazil, etc.).

Color	Symbolic meaning
black	
blue	
green	
pink	
red	
white	
yellow	

II. Go over the sentences and explain the underlined phrases from the context.

1. We found the poor guy black and blue near the train tracks.

2. The rules we gave the kids were black and white. No answering the phone or the door.

3. My oldest brother was the black sheep in our family. He dropped out of school at fifteen.

4. The kids were caught red-handed stealing chocolate bars.

5. I always wanted to go to university, but now I wish I had time to get a job. Grass is always greener on the other side.

6. The food industry was given a green light to extend the use of these chemicals.

7. You can tell by her flower garden that Sheila has a green thumb.

8. I got a phone call from a long-lost cousin out of the blue last week.

9. My mom was tickled pink when my father brought roses home for her.

Animal Words and Their Associations

Human beings evolved from animals and they regard animals as their closest friends. People normally associate their own appearances, traits, actions or characters with some of the animals as they have lively images and conspicuous (显眼的) characteristics, so both in English and Chinese, there are numerous expressions and sayings containing animals.

Same Animals and Similar Associations in English and Chinese

It is not difficult to find that the same animals have similar or even the same associations in English and Chinese. For example:

1. Mrs. Martin trusted the lawyer until she realized that he was a wolf in sheep's clothing.

    马丁夫人原来很信任那个律师，后来才认清他是只披着羊皮的狼。

2. You stupid ass! How could you do a thing like that?!

    你这头蠢驴！怎么会干出那种事儿来？！

3. He doesn't have an idea of his own. He just parrots what others say.

    他没有自己的想法，只会鹦鹉学舌。

4. He is as sly as a fox. You've got to watch him.

   他像狐狸一样狡猾，你对他可要当心点儿。

Same Animals but Different Associations in English and Chinese

With different life experiences, practices and customs, English-speaking people and Chinese people often make different and even totally opposite associations for the same animals.

A. Owls

In English, owls enjoy the status of being the symbol of wisdom, thus there is the expression "as wise as an owl". In Britain, there is a nursery rhyme (童谣) that goes like this: "A wise old owl lived in an oak. The more he saw, the less he spoke. The less he spoke, the more he heard. Why can't we all be like that wise old bird?"

However, the owl is associated with bad luck in Chinese culture. It even has got a nickname "夜猫子", thus there is "夜猫子进宅，凶事自来" (Bad things will happen when owls come to one's house). The mere sight of an owl or the sound of the bird's hooting is enough to cause people to draw back in fear.

B. Bats

Bats usually live in the dark and hence are considered blood-sucking creatures in English. Many sayings about bats are negative, such as "as blind as a bat" (瞎得跟蝙蝠一样，眼力不行，有眼无珠), "vampire bat" (吸血蝙蝠), "crazy as bat" (疯得像蝙蝠), "bats in the belfry" (发痴，异想天开), etc.

In Chinese culture, however, bats are regarded as auspicious (吉利的) animals and represent longevity (长寿) and happiness, mainly because the Chinese word for bat is "蝙蝠" (bianfu) which sounds very similar to "福" (fu, happiness, blessing, good fortune). Therefore, bats frequently appear in many traditional Chinese designs, for example "福寿双全" (Bats and peaches together mean enjoying both happiness and longevity) on Chinese New Year's paintings.

C. Dogs

Dogs are very common animals kept by people as pets or to guard buildings, but their connotations are quite different in English and Chinese. In Western culture, dogs are often called man's best friend since they are valued for their loyalty and devotion. Many expressions about them stress their positive qualities: "top dog" (头儿; 有权势的人), "a lucky dog" (幸运儿), "every dog has its day" (人人都有得意时), "love me, love my dog" (爱屋及乌). Of course, English-speaking people do not always speak of dogs endearingly. "You dog!", "son of a bitch" are fairly common swear words (脏话) in English.

In Chinese culture, though qualities like loyalty and dependability are admitted in the saying "狗不嫌家贫" (Dogs show no aversion to poor families), dogs are most often associated with unpleasantness. Most of the expressions about them are derogatory, for example, "狗仗人势" (to play the bully with the backing of a powerful person), "狗眼看人低" (one is so snobbish that he looks down upon ordinary people), "狗咬狗，一嘴毛" (bad people fighting each other, they will come to no good end), "狗逮耗子，多管闲事" (to poke one's nose into other people's business), etc.

Similar Associations but Different Animals in English and Chinese

Cultural differences make people associate the same animals with different meanings. Meanwhile, people in two different societies may associate different animals with similar characteristics.

A. Lions and Tigers

In Western countries, the most consistent depiction of the lion is in keeping with its image of "king of the jungle" or "king of the beasts", hence lions are popular symbols of royalty and stateliness (威严) and a symbol of bravery. They have been widely used in sculpture (雕塑) and statuary to provide a sense of majesty（威严）and awe（敬畏）, especially on public buildings.

The tiger is a very special animal in Chinese culture. The pattern on the forehead of a tiger is very similar to the Chinese character which means "king", so Chinese people believe that the tiger must be the natural-born king. Throughout Chinese history, the tiger has incited a sense of awe and admiration. It is regarded as an emblem of dignity, ferocity（凶猛）, sternness（严厉）and courage. Therefore, the tiger is often used as a metaphor for "great people" in China. It is common to find "tiger" in people's names. Traditionally, children would wear hats and shoes with the design of a tiger's head for the belief that tigers would protect them from evils.

B. Rabbits and Rats

In English, hares and rabbits are considered very shy. So when we talk about "timidness", there is "as timid as a hare/rabbit", yet Chinese people use "胆小如鼠"（literally meaning as timid as a rat）to describe someone who is very timid or always acts cautiously.

C. Horses and Oxen

In English, horses are often referred to as diligent, so when talking about diligence or hard work, there are "as strong as a horse", "to work like a horse" and "horsepower". Yet there are expressions like "俯首甘为孺子牛" (willing to serve others just like an ox), "老黄牛" (hard-working old ox), "力大如牛" (as strong as an ox), which illustrate the hard-working spirit of the ox in Chinese. The English saying "you can lead a horse to water but you cannot make it drink" is partly corresponding to "强按牛头不喝水" in Chinese.

In addition to the above-mentioned animals and their associations, there are some other expressions that have similar meanings. For example, "as mute as fish" and "噤若寒蝉", "donkey in a lion's hide" and "狐假虎威", "to kill the goose that lays golden eggs" and "杀鸡取卵", "to teach a pig to play on the flute" and "赶鸭子上架", "to shed crocodile tears" and "猫哭老鼠假慈悲", "like a duck to water" and "如鱼得水", "When the cat is away, the mice will play" and "山中无老虎，猴子称大王".

(Source: Huang Yucai, *A New Comparison of English and Chinese Languages and Cultures*)

Reflecting and Discussing

Match the idioms about animals on the left with their meanings on the right.

1. ants in one's pants
2. straw that breaks the camel's back
3. to let the cat out of the bag
4. Don't count your chickens before they are hatched.
5. a sitting duck
6. as poor as a church mouse
7. hen party
8. to look a gift horse in the mouth
9. a lion's share
10. Monkey see, monkey do.

a) party for only women
b) the greater portion
c) to be very restless and impatient
d) having bad manners when accepting a gift
e) That which is seen is copied.
f) an easy mark
g) Don't assume you have something until you really have it.
h) the thing to push you over the edge
i) very poor
j) telling something that has been a secret

Text B: How Ten Years in China Changed Me Forever

Read Text B and do the exercises online.

Unit 3 Perception and Culture

 Case Study

Discuss with your classmates the questions according to each case.

 Case 1

An Authentic Chinese Meal

Martin is an American student studying at Jinan University in Guangzhou. Wang Ying, Martin's classmate and four other Chinese students decided to treat Martin to an authentic Chinese meal in their dormitory.

However, when Martin was presented with the dinner, he was almost terrified by some of the food: pork stomach soup, pig liver with ginger and spring onion, chicken with mushrooms in which the chicken had been cut to pieces with bones attached to the meat.

Fortunately, there were courses like stirred fried beef, braised tofu and some vegetables that Martin loved. So he tried hard to use the Chinese chopsticks and stick to those dishes. Yet, Wang Ying kept putting the food he didn't like on his plate. When Wang asked how he loved the liver, Martin said, "It's very unusual... and interesting." This seemed to make Wang happy, and she gave him more liver. Martin tried to stop her, but she would not be stopped. Martin was so frustrated that he told her that he didn't really like it that much.

"But you said it was unusual and interesting!" Wang said.

"Well, they both mean something less than positive." Martin said carefully, trying not to hurt their feelings.

Wang then said, "So you don't like the food?"

"I'm not used to eating liver. That's all. But I do like the chicken, the beef, the tofu and the vegetables. I have had more than enough to eat." Martin was eager to let them know how much he appreciated their effort. He found a piece of chicken that was less bony, held it to his hands and ate it, and then licked his fingers.

Wang and her classmates looked at each other in shock.

(Source: Huang Yucai, *A New Comparison of English and Chinese Languages and Cultures*)

1. Why did Wang Ying keep putting the food on Martin's plate? Is it polite and hospitable? Why or why not?

2. How do you understand the words "unusual" and "interesting"? What did Martin really mean by them? How did Wang Ying understand them?

3. Why did Martin hold a piece of chicken in his hands and lick his fingers after eating it?

 Case 2

The Concept of Money

While I was studying in America, I met an American classmate named Jimmy. One day I was eager to buy a book, but I did not have enough money, so I borrowed three dollars from him. Before he lent me the three dollars, Jimmy asked me three times, "Are you sure you will return the money to me?" Four days later, he kept reminding me about the loan until I paid him back the money.

Interestingly enough, weeks later he borrowed $30 from me and said he would pay me back in a week. After one month, there was no sign of the money so I reminded him. To my surprise, he said, "I'm sorry, why didn't you remind me earlier?" and returned the money instantly.

(Source: Huang Yucai, *A New Comparison of English and Chinese Languages and Cultures*)

1. If you were "I" in this case, how would you perceive Jimmy's words and behavior when he lent and borrowed money to and from me? Is he rude and impolite?

2. What would be Jimmy's response if you were generous and said, "Don't mention it again. You don't have to pay me back."?

Unit 4　Barriers to Intercultural Communication

Prejudice is the child of ignorance.

—William Hazlitt

种族主义是美国难以根除的社会毒瘤。

——《光明日报》

Learning Objectives

Upon completion of this unit, you will be able to:

- Understand why ethnocentrism, stereotypes, prejudice and discrimination are barriers to intercultural communication.
- Define such terms as *ethnocentrism*, *stereotypes*, *prejudice* and *discrimination*.
- Gain an insight into your own ethnocentrism by GENE Scale.
- Increase your understanding about the rising racial discrimination against Asians in the United States and the reasons behind the sentiment amid the coronavirus pandemic.
- Understand, interpret and critically evaluate different cultural behavior.

 Lead-in

Read the following story and try to fill in each of the blanks with an appropriate word in the box.

How to Get Them to Jump?

```
chic
command
forbidden
insured
revolutionary
sporting
```

Some years ago, several international businessmen were on a conference cruise (乘船游览) when the ship began to sink. "Go, tell those fellows to put on life jackets and jump overboard," the captain directed his first mate (大副).

A few minutes later the first mate returned. "Those guys won't jump," he reported.

"Take over," the captain ordered, "and I'll see what I can do."

Unit 4 Barriers to Intercultural Communication

Returning moments later, he announced, "They're gone."

"How'd you do it?" asked the first mate.

I told different things to different people. I told the Englishman it was the _____ thing to do, and he jumped. I told the Frenchman it was _____; the German that it was a _____; the Italian that it was _____; the Russian that it was _____; so they all jumped overboard."

"And how did you get the American to jump?"

"No problem." said the captain, "I told him he was _____!"

(Source: Xu Lisheng, *Intercultural Communication in English*)

Questions for Intercultural Understanding

1. If there had been a Chinese businessman on board, what should the captain say to make him jump overboard?

2. What do you think of the story? Does it tell you something that is true of people from those different nations?

Barriers to Effective Intercultural Communication

1   Communication does not always result in an understanding because it is a symbolic behavior. People from different cultures **encode** and **decode** messages differently, increasing the chances of misunderstanding. The interpretation of the message, verbal or nonverbal, is based on the communication participant's cultural background, which varies accordingly for each person. Every culture provides its members with rules specifying appropriate and inappropriate behavior. Miscommunication occurs when the receiver does not receive the sender's **intended** message. The greater the difference between the sender's and receiver's culture, the greater the problem will be in intercultural communication.

2   In intercultural settings, it is easy to become trapped by invisible walls or barriers to communication. Although these walls are hard to perceive, they are not imaginary. The only way to "escape" is to learn to notice them and avoid

making the communication mistakes that come from them. This article will explore the nature of four common barriers and examine their impact on the cultivation of cross-cultural communication.

Ethnocentrism

3   The word "ethnocentrism" **is derived from** two Greek words: "ethnos", which means nation, and "kentron", which means center of a circle. This suggests that *ethnocentrism* occurs when our nation is seen as the center of the world and the beliefs, values, norms, and practices of our own culture are taken as superior to those of others.

4   As has often been pointed out, ethnocentrism is often expressed in the way people draw their maps. The Chinese, who call their country *Zhong Guo* (中国), were convinced in ancient times that China was the center of the world. Similar beliefs were held by other nations. The British drew the Prime Meridian of longitude (本初子午线) to run through Greenwich (格林威治), near London. Europeans drew maps of the world with Europe at the center, and North Americans with the New World at the center.

5   Believing that one's own country and culture are good is not bad in itself. After all, it is necessary to believe in one's country and group in order to pass along the values that are seen as important. But ethnocentrism can also be extreme, to the point that one cannot believe that another culture's values are equally good or worthy. Ethnocentrism becomes a barrier when it prevents people from even trying to see things from the other person's point of view.

6   In contrast to ethnocentrism is the attitude of cultural relativism, sometimes called "ethnorelativism". It maintains that cultures can only be understood relative to one another; there is no absolute standard of rightness or goodness that can be applied to cultural behavior; cultural difference is neither good nor bad; it is just different. Each culture has its unique way of judging and comparing cultural **dissonance**. In other words, *ethnorelativism* involves the view that all cultures are of equal value and that the values and behavior of a culture can only be judged using that culture as a **frame of reference**.

Stereotypes

7   Another barrier to intercultural communication is stereotyping. *Stereotypes* are those overgeneralized and **oversimplified** beliefs we use to categorize a group of people. We have a tendency to make a claim that often goes beyond facts, with no **valid** basis. Stereotypes may be based on truth, but they are **exaggerated**

statements regarding our beliefs about what a group of people are or should be. For example, imagine that your wallet was stolen by a Brazilian when you were traveling in Brazil. The incident ruined your whole trip there. When you came back, your friends asked how your trip to Brazil was. You might have said, "Those Brazilians are thieves. They stole my wallet." This is an example of stereotyping.

8   We form stereotypes in three ways. First, we may categorize people or things by the most obvious characteristics they possess. For example, when a Japanese student was asked about her first impression of the U.S., she said, "Wow! Everything is big here." Second, we may apply **a set of** characteristics to a whole group of people. For example, we may hear someone say that "Germans eat sausages and drink beer." Third, we may give the same treatment to each member of the group. For example, we may hear people say "You are a Chinese. You must be good at math."

Prejudice

9   Stereotypes naturally develop from a set of oversimplified beliefs into a rigid attitude towards a group of people. Such an attitude based on **erroneous** beliefs or **preconceptions** is called *prejudice*. Stereotypes and prejudice often occur together. In other words, when we hold beliefs (stereotypes), for example, about Italians, we also tend to have prejudice toward them.

10   It is helpful to consider different kinds of prejudice. The most **blatant** prejudice is easy to see but is less common today. It is more difficult, however, to **pinpoint** less obvious forms of prejudice. For example, *tokenism* is a kind of prejudice shown by people who have negative feelings about members of a particular group but do not want to admit they are prejudiced. Examples of this are often found in the hiring practices of large organizations where women and minorities may be used as **tokens** to convince that their hiring practices are non-discriminatory. *Arms-length*[1] prejudice is when people engage in friendly, positive behavior toward members of another group in public and **semiformal** situations (**casual** friendships at work, interactions in large social gatherings or at lectures) but avoid closer contact (dating, attending intimate social gatherings).

11   Like stereotypes, prejudice, once established, is very difficult to **undo**. Because it operates at a subconscious level (we often aren't really aware of our prejudice), there has to be a very **explicit** motivation to change our ways of thinking. One Lewiston（路易斯顿）, Maine（缅因州）resident explained how she had to examine her own reactions as she **was tempted to** agree with others'

prejudicial statements about Somalis (索马里人), such as "They don't speak English. They don't work. They're uneducated." She thought about this, noted that most Somalis not only speak English but also speak three or four other languages, and wondered, "Now who's uneducated?" She also recognized that most Somalis worked very hard; they moved to Lewiston because they wanted work and a better life than they had before.

Discrimination

12　The behavior that results from stereotypes or prejudice—**overt** actions to **exclude**, avoid, or distance oneself from other groups—is called *discrimination*. Discrimination may be based on racism or any other "ism" related to belonging to a cultural group (sexism, ageism, **elitism**). One way of thinking about discrimination is that power plus prejudice equals "ism". That is, if one belongs to a more powerful group and holds prejudice towards another less powerful group, the resulting actions towards members of that group can be called *discrimination*.

13　Discrimination may range from very **subtle** nonverbal cues (lack of eye contact, exclusion of someone from a conversation), to verbal **insults** and exclusion from job or other economic opportunities, to physical violence and even systematic **elimination** of a group, or **genocide**.

14　Ethnocentrism, stereotypes, prejudice and discrimination are not something we are born with. They are gradually developed from the process of learning and socialization and from our exposure to mass media. They may prevent us from interacting with people of different backgrounds; they may cause negative feelings during the interactions; and they can lead to unnecessary conflicts when they are **intense**. To overcome these barriers, it is suggested that empathy is the main communication skill we should learn. Empathic persons know how to show understanding by **projecting** themselves **onto** their partner's position. This means that to be empathic in intercultural interactions we need to be open-minded in terms of information sharing, to be imaginative in correctly drawing the picture of other's situations, and to show a commitment or strong willingness to understand our culturally different partners in any kind of situation.

　　(Source: Judith Martin & Thomas Nakayama, *Experiencing Intercultural Communication: An Introduction,* Chapter 2, and Guo-Ming Chen & William J. Starosta,

Unit 4 Barriers to Intercultural Communication

Foundations of Intercultural Communication, Chapter 3)

New Words

blatant	*adj.*	done in an obvious and open way without caring if people are shocked 明目张胆的，公然的
casual	*adj.*	without deep affection 感情不深的，疏远的
decode	*v.*	to attribute meaning to the messages or behavior generated by the sender 解码
discrimination	*n.*	the practice of treating sb. or a particular group in society less fairly than others 区别对待，歧视
dissonance	*n.*	lack of agreement 不和谐，不协调，不一致
elimination	*n.*	the act of removing or getting rid of sth. 消灭
elitism	*n.*	a way of organizing a system, society, etc. so that only a few people (= an elite) have power or influence 精英统治；精英主义
encode	*v.*	to change internal thoughts or feelings into verbal or nonverbal symbols in order to send messages 编码
erroneous	*adj.*	not correct; based on wrong information 错误的
exaggerated	*adj.*	describing sth. as better, larger etc. that it really is 夸张的，夸大的，言过其实的
exclude	*v.*	to prevent sb./sth. from entering a place or taking part in sth. 防止……进入，阻止……参加，把……排斥在外
explicit	*adj.*	said, done or shown in an open or direct way, so that you have no doubt about what is happening 直截了当的，不隐晦的
genocide	*n.*	the murder of a whole race or group of people 种族灭绝，大屠杀
insult	*n.*	a remark or an action that is said or done in order to offend sb. 辱骂，侮辱，冒犯
intended	*adj.*	that you are trying to achieve or reach sth. 意欲达到的，打算的

intense	*adj.*	very great or extreme in strength or degree 剧烈的，极度的
oversimplified	*adj.*	describing or explaining sth. in a way that is too simple and ignores many facts 过于简单化的
overt	*adj.*	done in an open way and not secretly 公开的，明显的
pinpoint	*v.*	to be able to give the exact reason for sth. or to describe sth. exactly 准确解释（或说明）
preconception	*n.*	an idea or opinion that is formed before you have enough information or experience 事先形成的观念，先入之见
prejudice	*n.*	an unreasonable dislike of or preference for a person, group, custom, etc., especially when it is based on their race, religion, sex, etc. 偏见，成见
semiformal	*adj.*	being or suitable for an occasion of moderate formality 半正式的
stereotype	*n.*	a fixed idea or image that many people have of a particular type of person or thing, but which is often not true in reality 模式化观念（或形象），老一套，刻板印象
subtle	*adj.*	not very noticeable or obvious 不易察觉的，不明显的，微妙的
token	*n.*	sth. that is a symbol of a feeling, a fact, an event, etc.（感觉、事实、事件等的）象征，标志；表示；信物
undo	*v.*	to cancel the effect of sth. 消除，取消，废止（某事的影响）
valid	*adj.*	based on what is logical or true 符合逻辑的，有根据的，确凿的

Useful Expressions

a set of	a group of similar things that belong together in some way 一套，一副，一组（类似的东西）
be derived from	to come or develop from sth. 衍生于，源自

Unit 4 Barriers to Intercultural Communication

be tempted to	to be attracted to do or have sth. 被诱惑，被引诱
frame of reference	a particular set of beliefs, ideas or experiences that affects how a person understands or judges sth.（影响人理解和判断事物的）信仰和准则
project oneself onto	to put oneself in a certain situation 将自己身处于

Cultural Note

1. Arms-length

Arms-length refers to a distance sufficient to exclude intimacy.

Reading Comprehension

I. Choose the best options to answer the following questions or fill in the blanks.

1. According to the text, which of the following is NOT a barrier to effective intercultural communication?
   A. Ethnocentrism.   B. Ethnorelativism.
   C. Stereotype.   D. Discrimination.

2. Which of the following statements is NOT true about "ethnocentrism" and "ethnorelativism"?
   A. Ethnocentrism occurs when one's own nation is seen as the center of the world.
   B. Ethnocentrism holds that the cultural beliefs, values, norms and practices of one's nation are superior to others.
   C. Ethnorelativism, or cultural relativism, can be extreme sometimes, denying that another culture's values are equally good or worthy.
   D. Ethnorelativism maintains that all cultures are of equal value and worth.

3. According to the text, which of the following is an example of "stereotyping"?
   A. Germans like eating sausages and drinking beer.
   B. You are Chinese. You must be good at martial arts（武术）.
   C. Everything is big in the U.S.
   D. All of the above.

4. The reference to "tokenism" in Paragraph 10 is intended to illustrate that _____.

   A. it's difficult to distinguish stereotypes from prejudice
   B. prejudice tends to be less explicit today
   C. people are more willing to engage themselves in large social gatherings rather than private ones
   D. women and minorities may be used as tokens in the hiring practices of large organizations

5. Which of the following is NOT an illustration of "discrimination"?

   A. Close eye contact.   B. Verbal insults.
   C. Rejection of women job applicants.   D. Genocide.

6. The author suggests that _____ is the most essential to overcome the barriers to intercultural communication.

   A. empathy   B. sensitivity
   C. openness   D. inclusiveness

7. Which of the following is the closest in meaning to the statement below?

   "Empathic persons know how to show understanding by projecting themselves onto their partner's position." (Paragraph 14)

   A. Empathic people are more willing to interact with other people.
   B. Empathic people are more willing to understand others from their cultural perspective.
   C. Empathic people tend to be more extroverted (外向的).
   D. Empathic people are more eager to socialize with people.

II. **Decide whether the following statements are TRUE, FALSE, or NOT GIVEN according to the information given in the text.**

   1. The word "ethnocentrism" originates from the Greek words "ethnos" and "kentron".

Unit 4 Barriers to Intercultural Communication

2. Ethnorelativism, or cultural relativism, holds that cultural difference is neither good or bad—it's just different.

_____

3. Stereotypes refer to the overgeneralized or oversimplified beliefs we tend to use to categorize different groups of people.

_____

4. Stereotypes and prejudice do not often occur together.

_____

5. Both stereotypes and prejudice are difficult to get rid of once established.

_____

6. Nonverbal insults are more likely to occur than verbal ones in actual intercultural communication.

_____

7. Humans are born with such tendencies as ethnocentrism, stereotypes, prejudice and discrimination.

_____

Checking Basic Concepts

Complete the following statements with a proper word in the box. Each word can be used only once.

ageism	discrimination	empathy
ethnocentrism	ethnorelativism	prejudice
racism	sexism	stereotyping

1. _____ occurs when our nation is seen as the center of the world and the beliefs, values, norms, and practices of our own culture are taken as superior to those of others.

2. If you believe that there is no absolute standard of rightness or goodness that can be applied to cultural behavior, you hold the attitude of _____.

3. "Americans are always in a hurry" is an example of _____.

4. _____ is a rigid attitude (usually negative) towards a cultural group based on little or no evidence.

5. _____ are behavior resulting from stereotypes or prejudice that cause some people to be denied equal participation or rights based on cultural group membership (such as race).

6. The unfair treatment of people because they are considered too old is called _____.

7. _____ refers to the prejudice, stereotyping, or discrimination, typically against women, on the basis of sex.

8. The "Black Lives Matter" movement is a protest against _____ in the U.S.

9. _____ is the ability to understand things from another person's perspective. It's the ability to share someone else's feelings and emotions and understand why they're having those feelings.

Language in Use

I. Complete the following sentences with the words in the box. Change the form if necessary. Each word can be used only once.

intend	insult	stereotype	exaggerate	explicit
token	casual	discrimination	intense	derive

1. Salesmen tend to _____ and overstate the effect and quality of their products in order to increase sales.

2. The questions were a(n) _____ to our intelligence.

3. He gave her an exquisite necklace on Valentine's Day as a(n) _____ of love.

Unit 4 Barriers to Intercultural Communication

4. The advertisements are _____ to improve the company's image.

5. Due to the quarrel, the friendship that was once considered to be "near and dear" between them has changed into something much more _____.

6. He gave me very _____ directions on how to get there.

7. A large number of words in modern English are _____ from the vocabulary of Latin.

8. He doesn't conform to the usual _____ of the businessman with a dark suit and briefcase.

9. Students nowadays are under huge pressure for the reason that the competition among them is becoming increasingly _____.

10. The government will legislate (立法) against _____ in the workplace to ensure that most job seekers can get equal opportunities.

II. Paraphrase the following sentences below from Text A.

1. The interpretation of the message, verbal or nonverbal, is based on the communication participant's cultural background, which varies accordingly for each person.

   _____
   _____
   _____

2. Discrimination may range from very subtle nonverbal cues (lack of eye contact, exclusion of someone from a conversation), to verbal insults and exclusion from job or other economic opportunities, to physical violence and even systematic eliminations of a group, or genocide.

   _____
   _____
   _____

Expanding Intercultural Knowledge

As discussed in Text A, ethnocentrism is the tendency to place one's own group (cultural, ethnic, or religious) in a position of centrality and highest worth, while creating negative attitudes and behavior toward other groups. Neuliep and McCroskey have developed the GENE (Generalized Ethnocentrism) Scale, which is designed to measure ethnocentrism. This scale and the directions for completing it are presented in the following Self-Assessment.

Self-Assessment: GENE Scale

Directions: The GENE Scale is composed of 22 statements concerning your feelings about your culture and other cultures. In the space provided to the left of each item, indicate the degree to which the statement applies to you by marking whether you (5) strongly agree, (4) agree, (3) are neutral, (2) disagree, or (1) strongly disagree with the statement. There are no right or wrong answers. Some of the statements are similar. Remember, everyone experiences some degree of ethnocentrism. Fortunately, ethnocentrism can be managed and reduced. Be honest! Work quickly and record your first response.

_____ 1. Most other cultures are backward compared to my culture.

_____ 2. My culture should be the role model for other cultures.

_____ 3. People from other cultures act strangely when they come into my culture.

_____ 4. Lifestyles in other cultures are just as valid as those in my culture.

_____ 5. Other cultures should try to be more like my culture.

_____ 6. I'm not interested in the values and customs of other cultures.

_____ 7. People in my culture could learn a lot from people of other cultures.

_____ 8. Most people from other cultures just don't know what's good for them.

_____ 9. I respect the values and customs of other cultures.

_____ 10. Other cultures are smart to look up to our culture.

_____ 11. Most people would be happier if they lived like people in my culture.

Unit 4 Barriers to Intercultural Communication

_____ 12. I have many friends from other cultures.

_____ 13. People in my culture have the best lifestyles of anywhere.

_____ 14. Lifestyles in other cultures are not as valid as those in my culture.

_____ 15. I'm very interested in the values and customs of other cultures.

_____ 16. I apply my values when judging people who are different.

_____ 17. I see people who are similar to me as virtuous.

_____ 18. I do not cooperate with people who are different.

_____ 19. Most people in my culture just don't know what is good for them.

_____ 20. I do not trust people who are different.

_____ 21. I dislike interacting with people from different cultures.

_____ 22. I have little respect for the values and customs of other cultures.

Scoring: To determine your ethnocentrism score, complete the following steps:

Step 1: Add your responses to Items 4, 7, and 9.

Step 2: Add your responses to Items 1, 2, 5, 8, 10, 11, 13, 14, 18, 20, 21, and 22 (note that not all items are used in scoring).

Step 3: Subtract the sum from Step 1 from 18 (i.e., 18 minus Step 1 sum).

Step 4: Add the results of Step 2 and Step 3. This sum is your generalized ethnocentrism score. Higher scores indicate higher ethnocentrism. Scores **above 55** are considered high ethnocentrism.

(Source: James W. Neuliep, *Intercultural Communication: A Contextual Approach*)

East Meets West

Liu Yang, a Chinese-born German artist, made some brilliant illustrations to show the cultural differences between the East and the West. Do you agree with the following graphic or symbolic **cultural stereotypes** between the East (pictures on the right) and the West (pictures on the left)? Which ones do you agree with and which ones do you disagree with? Give critical comments.

Three meals

Attitude toward punctuality

The boss

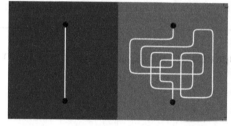
Size of the individual's ego

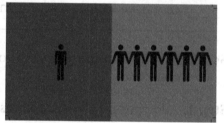
Self-expression

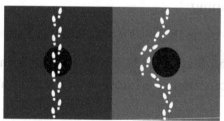
Life style

Problem-solving approach

Traveling

Sunshine

Shower time

Unit 4 Barriers to Intercultural Communication

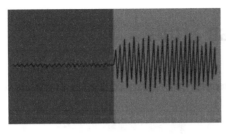
Noise level inside a restaurant

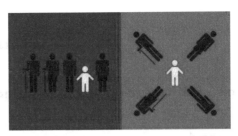
The child

Elderly in daily life

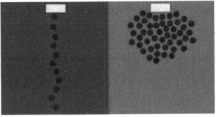
Standing in line

(Source: Liu Yang, *East Meets West*)

Text B

Increasing Racial Discrimination Against Asians Exposes Overall Racist Nature of U.S. Society

Read **Text B** and do the exercises online.

# Case Study

Discuss with your classmates the questions according to each case.

 Case 1

Family Life

Rosaline and Merita are from two different cultures. They are talking about one aspect of family life.

Rosaline: I think it's terrible that in your country children leave their parents when they are so young. Something that shocks me even more is that many parents want their children to leave home. I can't understand why children and parents don't like each other in your country.

Merita: In your country parents don't allow their children to become independent. Parents keep their children protected until they get married. How are young people in your country supposed to learn about life that way?

(Source: Wang Rong & Zhang Ailin, *Bridge Between Minds: Intercultural Communication*)

1. Where do you think they are from? Whom do you agree with? Why?
2. What attitude do they hold while talking about family life in another culture?
3. What harm does such an attitude usually bring to communication across cultures? How should we try to reduce its negative impact?

 Case 2

Mr. Bias's Decision

Mr. Bias is the director of a small private company. He is interviewing candidates for the position of assistant manager. He selects a bright and ambitious applicant. Later, he discovers that this applicant is from the country of Levadel (a fictitious nation). Since he thinks all Levadelians are stupid and lazy, he decides to select someone else for this position.

(Source: Wang Rong & Zhang Ailin, *Bridge Between Minds: Intercultural Communication*)

Unit 4 Barriers to Intercultural Communication

1. What do you think of Mr. Bias's decision?

2. What mistake does he make?

3. Have you ever made such mistakes in your own life? How can you avoid them when interacting with people from a different cultural background?

Unit 5 Identity and Culture

Life isn't about finding yourself. Life is about creating yourself.

—*George B. Shaw*

知人者智,自知者明。

——《道德经》

Learning Objectives

Upon completion of this unit, you will be able to:

- Understand the nature of identity.
- Define such terms as *personal identities* and *social identities*.
- Explain different dimensions of your social identities.
- Discuss the impact of culture on identities.
- Understand the dark side of identity.
- Assess the importance of your identities.
- Understand, interpret and critically evaluate different cultural identities.

 Lead-in

Who Am I?

Growing up as a former Jehovah's Witness (耶和华信徒), color or ethnicity was not something that really was part of my focus in life. Although being biracial (双种族的)—half Croatian (克罗地亚人) and half Jamaican (牙买加人)—was part of my heritage, it did not have an impact on my life. Religion was my core identity and belief system. It wasn't until my freshman year in high school during a math class that I really understood that there was a bigger world of distinction. A fellow student turned to me during class and blurted out (脱口而出), "Oh my god, Alex—You are black!" At that moment, I realized that I did not really know what that meant. Growing up in a predominantly (大多数地) white neighborhood and constantly being surrounded by my mother's Eastern European friends and other Jehovah's Witnesses, I had limited experience and a lack of emotional connection to my black side. As a result, throughout my life, I have become used to people trying to fit me into a category or a box I don't fit in. I see myself as a collage (拼贴画) of collided identities but, one whole: Me!

(Source: Stella Ting-Toomey & Leeva C. Chung, *Understanding Intercultural Communication*)

Questions for Intercultural Understanding

1. Can you use some words to describe who Alex is?

2. Have you ever thought about who you are? Could you use as many words as possible to define yourself?

3. Do you know who you are in other people's eyes? Do they see you in the same or similar way as you see yourself?

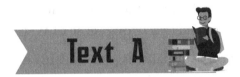

Cultural Identity: Issues of Belonging

1   When we ask ourselves, "Who am I?", "How is my identity formed and maintained?", and "Who am I in relationship to others?", we are asking questions of identity. The answers we come up with in response to these **queries** provide **a roll call of** identity considerations.

2   Identity, then, is defined by our "knowing" of ourselves. This knowing means taking an **inventory** of who we are. Part of that inventory involves our concepts of ourselves as unique individuals—our *personal identities* (for example, whether we are shy, athletic, or interested in soccer). Part of the inventory involves our role identities (for example, work or professional roles), relational identities (for example, enemies, family members, lovers), and our membership in groups (such as national, religious or political groups, social organizations, or regional identities). These latter, group-based aspects of identity make up our *social identities*. Social identity is where the individual meets larger collective bodies, or groups of **affiliation**. This can raise many interesting issues as people struggle to define groups and how groups impact individuals.

Examples of Social Identity

3   We use the terms "identity" and "identities" interchangeably, in that one's identity actually consists of multiple identities acting **in concert**. As the situation varies, people may choose to emphasize one or more of their identities. At work, one's occupational and organizational identities are **paramount**, but when visiting parents, a person is first a son or a daughter. In both environments, however,

other identities, such as race and biological sex, are also present, although in a secondary role. In this text, we will briefly examine a few of people's many identities and illustrate how culture influences each.

Racial Identity

4   The concept grew out of efforts by eighteenth-century European anthropologists to place people into different categories based largely on their outward appearance. During that era, race was also used as a device for justifying European dominance over Africans and American Indians. **In retrospect**, it is easy to see how those early endeavors were influenced by feelings of prejudice and ethnocentrism grounded in a strong sense of Western superiority.

5   Today, *racial identity* is usually associated with external physical traits such as skin color, hair **texture**, facial appearance, and eye shape. Modern science, however, has found that there is very little **genetic** variation among human beings, which undermines the belief that race can be used to categorize people. The idea has been further **eroded** by centuries of genetic intermixing, which is becoming an increasing occurrence in **contemporary** society through intercultural marriage. Although race remains a commonly used term in the United States, it is often interchanged with the term "ethnic group".

Ethnic Identity

6   As just stated above, racial identity is traditionally tied to one's biological ancestry that produces similar physical characteristics. *Ethnicity* or *ethnic identity*, on the other hand, is derived from a sense of shared heritage, history, traditions, values, similar behavior and area of origin.

7   The ethnicity of many U.S. Americans is tied to their ancestors' home of origin before immigrating to the United States, such as Germany, Italy, Mexico, China, or other places. Generations **subsequent** to the original immigrants often refer to themselves using terms such as "German-American", "Italian-American", or "Chinese-American". The **hyphen** both separates and connects the two cultural traditions.

8   During the formative years of the United States, immigrants often grouped together in a particular region to form ethnic communities, and some of these continue today, such as Chinatown in San Francisco[1] and Little Italy in New York[2]. In these areas, people's sense of ethnic identity tends to remain strong. But as time passes, members of younger generations tend to move to areas of greater ethnic diversity and frequently marry into other ethnic groups. For some, this

can **dilute** their feelings of ethnic identity.

Gender Identity

9   *Gender identity* is quite different from biological sex or sexual identity. Gender is a socially constructed concept that refers to how a particular culture differentiates **masculine** and **feminine** social roles.

10   What constitutes displays of gender identity varies across cultures and is constantly changing, often in language. In Japanese, certain words are traditionally used exclusively by women, while men employ entirely different words to express the same meaning. In English, there is little or no distinction between words used by women and those used by men.

11   A culture's gender norms can also influence career decisions. For instance, males represent less than 6 percent of nurses in the United States. This is because most people consider nursing to be a woman's career.

National Identity

12   *National identity* refers to nationality, which the majority of people associate with the nation where they were born. But national identity can also be acquired by immigration. People who have taken citizenship in a country different from their birthplace may eventually begin to adopt some or all aspects of a new national identity, depending on the strength of their attachment to their new homeland.

13   **Alternatively**, people residing permanently in another nation may retain a strong connection to their homeland. National identity usually becomes more **pronounced** when people are away from their home country. When asked where they are from, international travelers normally respond with their national identity—e.g., "We are from Canada."

Regional Identity

14   With the exception of very small nations, every country can be divided into a number of different geographical regions, and often those regions reflect varying cultural traits. The cultural contrasts among these regions may be **manifested** through ethnicity, language, accent, dialect, customs, food, dress, or different historical and political **legacies**. Residents of these regions use one or more of those characteristics to demonstrate their *regional identity*. In China, certain languages like Mongolian and Tibetan, or dialects such as Hakka and Cantonese are unintelligible to non-locals.

Cyber Identity

15   The Internet provides an opportunity to escape the constraints of everyday identities. People can **alter** their style of being just slightly or **indulge in** wild experiments with their identity by changing their age, history, personality, physical appearance, even their gender. The username they choose, the details they do or don't indicate about themselves, the information presented on their personal web page, the **persona** or avatar[3] they assume in an online community—all are important aspects of how people demonstrate their *cyber identity*.

16   There are many other forms of identity that play a significant role in the daily lives of people. For example, we have not examined the functions of age, religion, political affiliation, socio-economic class, physical ability, or minority status, all of which are part of most individuals' identity and are influenced by culture. However, the various identities discussed here should give you an awareness of the complexity of the topic and of how culture and communication influence identity.

17   In the contemporary world, multiple cultural identities are becoming more commonplace. The globalized economy, immigration, ease of foreign travel, communication technologies, and intercultural marriage are bringing about an increased mixing of cultures, and this mixing is producing people who possess multiple cultural identities. But regardless of how they are achieved, the form they take, or how they are acquired, people's identities will remain a product of culture.

Dark Side of Identity

18   It should be clear that, fundamentally, identity is about similarities and differences. In other words, you identify with something as a result of preference, understanding, familiarity, or socialization. You will likely have greater tolerance toward the people and things you prefer, understand, and find familiar. But by definition, intercultural communication involves people from dissimilar cultures, and this makes difference a **normative** condition. Thus your reaction to, and ability to manage, those differences are key to successful intercultural interactions. A preference for things you understand and are familiar with can **adversely** influence your perception of, and attitude towards, new and different people and things. This can lead to stereotyping, prejudice, racism, and ethnocentrism.

(Source: John R. Baldwin et al., *Intercultural Communication for Everyday Life*, Chapter 5 and Larry A. Samovar et al., *Communication Between Cultures*, Chapter 7)

Unit 5 Identity and Culture

 New Words

adversely	adv.	in a way that is negative and unpleasant and not likely to produce a good result 不利地，有害地；反面地
affiliation	n.	one group or organization's official connection with another 隶属，从属
alter	v.	to become different; to make sb./sth. different（使）改变，更改，改动
alternatively	adv.	used to introduce a suggestion that is a second choice or possibility 或者，二者选一地
contemporary	adj.	marked by characteristics of the present period 现代的，当代的，当时的
dilute	v.	to make sth. weaker or less effective 削弱，降低，使降低效果
erode	v.	to gradually destroy or be gradually destroyed 逐渐破坏
feminine	adj.	having the qualities or appearance considered to be typical of women; connected with women（指气质或外貌）女性特有的，女性的，妇女的
genetic	adj.	connected with genes (the units in the cells of a living thing that control its physical characteristics) or genetics (the study of genes) 基因的，遗传学的
hyphen	n.	the mark (-) used to join two words together to make a new one, or to show that a word has been divided between the end of one line and the beginning of the next 连字符
inventory	n.	a list of traits, preferences, attitudes, interests, or abilities used to evaluate personal characteristics or skills 列表，清单
legacy	n.	sth. handed down from an ancestor or a predecessor or from the past 遗产；传承下来的事务
manifest	v.	to show sth. clearly, especially a feeling, an attitude or a quality 表明，清楚显示（尤指情感、态度或品质）
masculine	adj.	having the qualities or appearance considered to be typical of men; connected with or like men 阳刚的，男人的，像男人的

normative	*adj.*	describing or setting standards or rules of behavior 规范的，标准的
paramount	*adj.*	more important than anything else 至为重要的，首要的
persona	*n.*	the aspects of a person's character shown to other people, especially when his/her real character is different 人设，人格面具
pronounced	*adj.*	very noticeable, obvious or strongly expressed 显著的，很明显的；表达明确的
query	*n.*	a question, especially one asking for information or expressing a doubt about sth. 疑问，询问
subsequent	*adj.*	happening after sth. else 随后的，后来的，之后的
texture	*n.*	the way a surface, substance or piece of cloth feels when you touch it, for example, how rough, smooth, hard or soft it is 质地，手感
unintelligible	*adj.*	impossible to understand 难以理解的，难懂的

Useful Expressions

a roll call of	a list of a particular type of people or things 一连串的……
in concert	together, in cooperation 共同，协作
in retrospect	thinking about a past event or situation, often with a different opinion of it from the one you had at the time 回顾，回想，追溯往事
indulge in	to allow yourself to have or do sth. that you like, especially sth. that is considered bad for you 沉湎，沉迷，沉溺于……

Cultural Notes

1. Chinatown in San Francisco

Chinatown（中国城）in San Francisco is the oldest one in North America and covers 24 city blocks and is also the most densely populated neighborhood west of Manhattan. This neighborhood is one of the most popular attractions in San Francisco. The residents are almost all Chinese and often speak little English.

Unit 5 Identity and Culture

2. Little Italy in New York

Little Italy in New York is a must-see neighborhood in Downtown Manhattan and is popular with most New York tourists. It is the area where the first Italian immigrants settled and is lively and full of the Italian way of life. New York's Little Italy is currently being taken over by Chinatown and other neighborhoods and is becoming smaller and smaller in size.

3. avatar

In the text, avatar (网络虚拟人物形象代名词) is an electronic image that represents and may be manipulated by a computer user (as in a game). For example, she chose a penguin as her personal avatar in the chat room. The word originates from the incarnation (化身) of a Hindu deity (印度教的神). It is often used as an embodiment (as of a concept or philosophy) in a person. For example, she was regarded as an avatar of charity and concern for the poor.

Reading Comprehension

I. Choose the best options to answer the following questions or fill in the blanks.

1. According to the text, "identity" can be defined as _____.
   A. a person's self-definition as a unique individual in behavior, attitudes, and beliefs
   B. the concept of who we are
   C. our membership in groups
   D. all of the above

2. "Social identities" can be based on all of the following EXCEPT _____.
   A. relations in a family   B. one's personal traits
   C. social roles   D. membership in groups

3. Which of the following identities is **NOT** discussed in the text?
   A. Racial identity.   B. Ethnic identity.
   C. Cyber identity.   D. Religious identity.

4. According to the text, "ethnic identity" is derived from a sense of shared _____.
   A. biological ancestry   B. genetic characteristics
   C. heritage and traditions   D. physical traits

5. "Gender identity" is associated with _____.
   A. biological sex   B. ethnic identity
   C. masculine or feminine social roles D. mother tongue

6. Which of the following is an example of "regional identity"?
   A. Italian.   B. Asian.
   C. Southerner.   D. Christian.

7. How is identity displayed online?
   A. By the username you choose.
   B. By the details you disclose about yourself.
   C. By the images you share.
   D. All of the above.

II. Decide whether the following statements are TRUE, FALSE, or NOT GIVEN according to the information given in the text.

1. Personal identity is what sets you apart from other social members and marks you as special or unique.

2. Social identity is about whether we are shy, athletic, or interested in soccer, etc.

3. The fact that there's very little genetic variation among human beings weakens the belief that race can be used to categorize people.

4. One's social identity is more important than his or her personal identity.

5. Racial identity and ethnic identity are the same thing.

6. Gender identity is not different from biological sex or sexual identity.

7. One can have both a national and a regional identity at the same time.

8. A preference for one's own culture might result in cultural issues such as stereotyping or ethnocentrism.

Unit 5 Identity and Culture

Checking Basic Concepts

Complete the following statements with a proper phrase in the box. Each phrase can be used only once.

cyber identity	personal identity	ethnic identity
racial identity	gender identity	regional identity
national identity	social identity	

1. _____ involves our concepts of ourselves as unique individuals.

2. Where the individual meets larger collective bodies, or groups of affiliation is known as one's _____.

3. One's biological ancestry that produces similar physical characteristics such as skin color, hair texture, facial appearance, and eye shape is associated with his or her _____.

4. _____ refers to the ethnic group with which an individual most closely associates. Identifying it is not as simple as checking a box according to one's skin color.

5. Different from biological sex, _____ is linked to how a particular culture differentiates masculine and feminine social roles.

6. The majority of people associate their _____ with the nation where they were born. They can also acquire it by immigration.

7. Accent, dialect, customs, food and dress demonstrate people's _____.

8. A(n) _____ is all of the things that make you "you" on your online profiles: all of your comments, your usernames, and interactions online.

Language in Use

I. **Complete the following sentences with the words in the box. Change the form if necessary. Each word can be used only once.**

| query | retrospect | pronounced | adverse |
| paramount | alter | indulge | subsequent |

1. Parents can rest assured (放心) that their children's safety will be of _____ importance.

2. If you have a(n) _____ about the explanation of cultural identity, you can resort to more reference books to get a deeper understanding of it.

3. Due to global warming, researchers have found that the rise of sea level is most _____ near the poles.

4. Those who are overweight or _____ in high-salt diets are prone to (倾向于) suffer from high blood pressure.

5. In _____, I wish that I had thought about alternative courses of action.

6. Economic recession (衰退) and the competition for jobs could greatly _____ current social situation.

7. This drug is known to have _____ side effects.

8. Developments on this issue will be dealt with in a(n) _____ report.

II. Paraphrase the following sentences from Text A.

1. As the situation varies, people may choose to emphasize one or more of their identities. At work, one's occupational and organizational identity are paramount, but when visiting parents, a person is first a son or a daughter.

2. A preference for things you understand and are familiar with can adversely influence your perception of, and attitude toward, new and different people and things. This can lead to stereotyping, prejudice, racism, and ethnocentrism.

Unit 5 Identity and Culture

Expanding Intercultural Knowledge

Assessing the Importance of Your Social and Personal Identities

Instructions: The following items describe how people think about themselves and communicate in various situations. Let your first response be your guide and circle the number in the scale that best reflects your overall value. The following scale is used for each item:

4 = SA = strongly agree—IT'S ME!

3 = MA = moderately agree—It's kind of like me.

2 = MD = moderately disagree—It's kind of not me.

1 = SD = strongly disagree—IT'S NOT ME!

		SA	MA	MD	SD
1.	My group memberships (e.g., ethnic or gender) are important when I communicate with others.	4	3	2	1
2.	My personality usually comes across loud and clear when I communicate.	4	3	2	1
3.	I am aware of my own ethnic background or social roles when I communicate.	4	3	2	1
4.	My personality has a stronger influence on my everyday interaction than any social role.	4	3	2	1
5.	I am aware of ethnic or gender role differences.	4	3	2	1
6.	I tend to focus on the unique characteristics of the individual when I communicate.	4	3	2	1
7.	Some aspects of my ethnic or social roles always shape my communication.	4	3	2	1
8.	I believe my personal identity is much more important than any of my social membership categories.	4	3	2	1
9.	If people want to know me, they should pay more attention to my professional or student role identity.	4	3	2	1
10.	My unique self is more important to me than my ethnic or cultural role self.	4	3	2	1

Scoring:

Add up the scores on all the odd-numbered items and you will find your social identity score. **Social identity score:** _____.

Add up the scores on all the even-numbered items and you will find your personal identity score. **Personal identity score:** _____.

Interpretation: Scores on each identity dimension can range from 5 to 20; the higher the score, the more social and/or personal you are. If all the scores are similar on both identity dimensions, you emphasize the importance of both social and personal identities in your everyday communication process.

(Source: Stella Ting-Toomey & Leeva C. Chung, *Understanding Intercultural Communication*)

Reflecting and Discussing

1. In the first encounter with a stranger, do you usually try to understand the social role identity or personal identity of the stranger? Why?

2. Do you primarily share your social role identity or personal role identity information with a stranger? What factors (e.g., work situations, classroom situations, or relation with other communicators) usually prompt you to exchange either more social role data or more personal identity data in your communication process?

I Am Not Your Asian Stereotype

Read Text B and do the exercises online.

Unit 5　Identity and Culture

 Case Study

Discuss with your classmates the questions according to each case.

 Case 1

An Alienated Young Asian American

Communication scholar Kathleen Wong describes how she gradually became aware of the intersections（交集）of race, class, and ethnicity through her own life experiences. Her parents were Chinese immigrants and they worked in a factory. She entered an elite（精英）college where the students were mostly white and children of teachers, attorneys（律师）, doctors, and other professionals.

It took me many years to understand the many dimensions of alienation（疏离感）I felt as a young Asian American woman coming of age. I didn't understand the complexity and muddiness（混浊；混乱）of my own internalized oppression（压抑）that had rendered（使……变得）me silent about my Chinese American parents, their occupations and my working-class neighborhood…

I spent most of my undergraduate career in total culture shock entering an institution and community that was considerably whiter than the one in which I had grown up. I remember the familiar awkwardness of silence when asked about my parents' occupations… I found I had little in common with my Chinese American friends in terms of ethnic culture. Somehow I had grown up thinking our practices were those of Chinese immigrants universally. I had grown up paradoxically（自相矛盾地）aware of class and at the same time totally unaware of how my own ethnic culture was shaped by class… In trying to erase class, I was erasing my own ethnic and racial identity… with each new experience I understand more about the connectedness of the many parts of my identities and how these parts cannot be separated from one another.

(Source: Judith N. Martin & Thomas K. Nakayama, *Intercultural Communication in Contexts*)

1. As a young Chinese American, what did she think of her racial, ethnic and class identities? What made her feel like that?

2. From this case, could you figure out the dark side of identities?

Case 2

African American Identity: More Than DNA Tests

Commentator John McWhorter says he doesn't need a DNA analysis to know where he comes from. He says he's content with his family history the way it is: He's a black American, and he admires his ancestors.

When I was a little kid, I was reminded that I would never know exactly where in Africa my ancestors lived. But now with the wonders of modern science, all I have to do is hand over a scraping (皮屑) from my cheek and my DNA will be able to tell me whether I trace back to Senegal (塞内加尔), Angola (安哥拉) or somewhere in between. I suppose I'll sooner or later have it tested. But I can't say that I've ever felt like I didn't know where my roots were in the meantime because my roots are right here in the U.S.A.

Don't get me wrong. There is certainly nothing bad about tracing ourselves back further than plantation slavery. Yet I'm unable to join those who say that finding out their ancestors lived in Ghana (加纳) makes them feel complete or that they found home. As a matter of fact, I've always thought of myself as the descendant of Africans who made the best out of the worst. This leaves out the strength, the human spirit that's always burned bright in ordinary black people living lives of dignity.

Where do I come from? I come from a people who the very year I was born, 1965, had turned America upside down and gained the right to vote in the South. I come from my grandmother who was a child in Atlanta, and was a playmate of the very Martin Luther King who went on to gain us that Voting Rights Act.

What I come from is black American people. They produce no shame in me. They are my heroes. They are my home. They are enough.

(Source: Fan Weiwei, *A Multimedia Approach to Intercultural Communication*)

1. How did the commentator define his identity as an African-American?
2. In the global village, what can be done to avoid identity crisis?

Unit 6 Cultural Values

Mind is actually internalized culture.

—*Edward T. Hall*

能行五者于天下，为仁矣。此五者为：恭、宽、信、敏、惠。

——《论语》

Learning Objectives

Upon completion of this unit, you will be able to:

- Define such terms as *value* and *value orientation*.
- Understand how values form the core of a culture.
- Compare and evaluate value orientations critically.
- Understand *Kluckhohn and Strodtbeck's Value Orientation Model*.
- Understand *Hofstede-Bond Value Dimensions*.
- Analyze how value differences shape people's behavior across cultures.

 Lead-in

Proverbs and Values

Proverbs reflect values of the users. Study the following proverbs and decide what value(s) they represent.

1. Blood is thicker than water.
2. Too many cooks spoil the broth.
3. God helps those who help themselves.
4. Time is money.
5. A man's home is his castle.
6. Think before you leap.
7. Don't cry over the spilt milk.
8. A single arrow is easily broken, but not a bunch.

(Source: Wang Rong & Zhang Ailin, *Bridge Between Minds: Intercultural Communication*)

Unit 6 Cultural Values

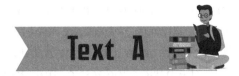

Values and Value Orientations Across Cultures

1 The concept of *values* generally refers to shared ideas about the desired ends of human life and the means to reach these goals. They usually express what is true and what is untrue, what is right and what is wrong, what is important and what is unimportant, and what is good and what is bad. They refer to the norms that **underlie** cultural patterns and guide the society in response to physical and social environments. However, values differ from culture to culture. The ways in which human beings in all cultures of the world deal with problems in terms of values are called *value **orientations***. Value orientations form the basic lenses through which we view not only our own actions but also the actions of others. They also serve as standards for how we should communicate appropriately with others and set the emotional tone for how we should interpret and evaluate the behavior of others. However, as each culture has its own system of **coherent**, consistent, and systematic understanding and interpretation of the world in its context, each has a unique set of value orientations.

2 Among the most influential and pioneering researches in this regard has been the work carried out by Kluckhohn and Strodtbeck[1] (1961) during the mid-twentieth century. In their study, they **posit** five main orientations that all cultures must address: human nature orientation; relational orientation; people-nature orientation; activity orientation and time orientation. It is important to notice that these orientations are generalizations, and they are not always followed by all members of a cultural group.

Human Nature Orientation

3 Is human nature inherently good, bad, or in-between? Do our customs, behavior and social institutions express the belief that humans just need opportunities for virtue to **flourish**, or that humans need to be restrained lest **vice** and **wickedness** run wild? As a matter of fact, human nature is complicated. In many cultures, "**innately** good" and "innately evil" coexist, with different aspects emphasized in different ways and contexts.

4 According to the Confucian tradition, human nature is composed of **sympathy**, justice, respect, and wisdom. Human beings can come together

because of their commonly shared human nature. The essence is reflected in *Three-Character Classic*[2] as "Human beings are innately good. They draw close to one another by their common nature, but habits and customs keep them apart." This emphasis on the basic goodness of human nature is reflected in the Confucian practices of **self-cultivation** and moral education.

5   Some traditions within Christianity, on the other hand, while believing that human nature was originally good and that God has a plan to **redeem** human nature, place great emphasis on the present sinfulness and capacity for **depravity** in human nature. They believe that human nature has been **corrupted** and no aspect of the human person **is immune to** this corruption. Examples of Christian groups which share this view are the Calvinists（加尔文派）, among whom we can include the Puritans（清教徒）who colonized North America.

Relational Orientation

6   There are in general two kinds of cultural groups: some cultural groups are **in favor of** *individualism* whereas others are in favor of *collectivism*. Of course there are also some other kinds of cultural groups.

7   Individualist cultures tend to emphasize self-concept in terms of self-esteem, self-identity, self-awareness, self-image and self-expression. In other words, individuals are treated as the most important element in all social settings. In individualist cultures, personal goals are above group goals; "I" consciousness prevails and competition is encouraged. Individualism, as stated by Geert H. Hofstede[3] (2001), is the most important value held in the United States, Australia, Great Britain, Canada, the Netherlands, New Zealand, Italy, Belgium and Denmark.

8   In contrast to individualist cultures, collectivist cultures tend to emphasize the concept of collectivism or group rather than self-concept, "we" rather than "I" consciousness. That is, the group or in-group needs are emphasized. People in the collectivist cultures tend to be interrelated, interconnected and interdependent and show loyalty and conformity to the group's norms and values. In collectivist cultures, the interest of the group is viewed above the interest of the individual; authority is viewed as representing the group; interdependence and harmony rather than independence and **dichotomy**, cooperation rather than competition are highly valued in human interaction and communication. Collectivism, according to Hofstede, is held in Colombia, Venezuela（委内瑞拉）, Pakistan, Peru, China, Singapore, Chile（智利）, etc.

People-Nature Orientation

9   The harmony of humans with nature is one of the most significant contributions the Confucian tradition can offer to the building of a global community. The unity with nature that Confucians believe in also embraces the Earth. This vision is an ***anthropocosmic*** *world view*, in which the human **is embedded in** the cosmic order, rather than an ***anthropocentric*** *world view*, in which the human is an isolated individual, **alienated** from the natural world.

10   An anthropocentric world view **envisions** the human individual as the center of everything in the cosmos, and all others including nature are scaled or rated with the interest, freedom, and dignity of the individual as the reference. The Enlightenment[4] of the 17th and 18th centuries in Europe promoted the notion that knowledge is power. To dare to know, control, master, **dominate**, use and conquer nature to satisfy their individual needs, humans have to be equipped with reason and knowledge and use them as power in their exploration for nature. The attitude of looking at nature as an object contributed to the development of Western science and technology, and thus laid the foundation for the development of modernity. However, it has also brought about disadvantages, even destruction to the world, nature, and the human species.

Activity Orientation

11   *Activity orientation* is defined as how the people of a culture view human actions and how they express themselves through activities. Activity orientation falls into two groups: "doing" and "being". "Doing" orientation is closely connected with action, achievement, controlling and conquering nature, for example. "Being" orientation is closely connected with the harmony with nature and the building of **personhood**, which refers to the quality of being a good person who is concerned not only about his/her own self but also about others or a person who embodies the unity of humanity with heaven, earth, and the **myriad** things. It is also generally believed that Asian cultures prefer "being" orientation while Western cultures prefer "doing" orientation.

Time Orientation

12   A culture's conception of time, use of it and attitude toward it vary with cultures and reveal how the particular culture believes in and values it. There are three *time orientations*: past, present and future orientation. Some cultures tend to look back because they have a long history of which they can **boast**. They are past-oriented. Cultures that concentrate on the present and don't worry too

much about tomorrow are present-oriented. Most post-industrial cultures are future-oriented because they place a lot of emphasis on the future, striving to ensure that the future will be better than the present.

13   How to regulate time is also an important aspect of our time orientation. The regulation of time differs from culture to culture. According to Edward T. Hall (1976), there are two time cultures, namely, *M-time cultures* (**monochronic** time cultures) and *P-time cultures* (**polychronic** time cultures).

14   M-time is noted for its emphasis on schedules, **segmentation** and **promptness**. It features one event at a time. Time is perceived as a **linear** structure just like a ribbon **stretching** from the past into the future. It is perceived as something concrete, tangible, which can be saved, borrowed, sold, spent, wasted, lost, made up for, divided, killed, and measured. Northern American, Western and Northern European cultures are typical M-time cultures with the U.S.A., Germany, and Switzerland representing classic examples.

15   P-time practiced by most other peoples is less rigid and **clock-bound**. People from P-time cultures schedule several activities at the same time, and time for them is more flexible and more human-centered. Latin American, African, Arab and most Asian cultures are representatives of P-time patterns.

(Source: Jia Yuxin, *Experiencing Global Intercultural Communication*, Chapter 5)

New Words

alienate	v.	to make sb. feel that he/she does not fit in a particular group 使（与某群体）格格不入，使疏远
anthropocentric	adj.	believing that humans are more important than anything else 人类中心论的；人本位的
anthropocosmic	adj.	emphasizing the harmony between humankind and cosmos 天人和谐的
boast	v.	to talk with too much pride about sth. that you have or can do 自夸，自吹自擂
clock-bound	adj.	requiring completion by a specified deadline or within a specified period of time 有时限性的

coherent	*adj.*	(of ideas, thoughts, arguments, etc.) logical and well organized; easy to understand and clear（看法、思想、论点等）合乎逻辑的，有条理的，清楚易懂的
corrupt	*v.*	to degrade or debase by making errors or unintentional alterations 腐化，堕落
depravity	*n.*	the state of being morally bad 堕落，腐化
dichotomy	*n.*	a division or contrast between two things that are or are represented as being opposed or entirely different（对立或完全不同事物间的）区分，区别，对立
dominate	*v.*	to control; to rule 掌控；占主导地位
envision	*v.*	to imagine what a situation will be like in the future, especially a situation you intend to work towards; hold the opinion 展望；想象；认为
flourish	*v.*	(of a person, animal, or other living organism) to grow or develop in a healthy or vigorous way, especially as the result of a particularly favorable environment 茁长成长；繁盛
innately	*adv.*	connected with a quality or an ability that you were born with, not one you have learned 天生地，固有地；本质地
linear	*adj.*	(things) developing like lines extending from a beginning and to a single direction, no coming back（发展）直线式的
monochronic	*adj.*	performing tasks one at a time in a linear sequence 单一时间模式的
myriad	*adj.*	having a large number or great variety 大量的，各种各样的
orientation	*n.*	a person's basic beliefs or feelings about a particular subject（个人的）基本信仰；态度，观点
personhood	*n.*	the condition of being a person who is an individual with inalienable rights 人格

polychronic	*adj.*	performing elements of different tasks simultaneously 多元时间模式的
posit	*v.*	to put forth an idea for discussion 设定……以讨论
promptness	*n.*	the fact of being done, delivered etc. at once or without delay 即时性
redeem	*v.*	to make amends for (error or evil); do sth. that compensates for poor past performance or behavior（基督教中）救赎；挽回；弥补（过失）
segmentation	*n.*	the act of dividing sth. into different parts; one of these parts 分割，划分，分割成（或划分成）的部分
self-cultivation	*n.*	the development of one's mind or capacities through one's own efforts 修身，自我修养
stretch	*v.*	extend or draw out beyond ordinary or normal limits 延伸
sympathy	*n.*	the feeling of being sorry for sb.; showing that you understand and care about sb.'s problems 同情
underlie	*v.*	to be the basis or cause of sth. 构成……的基础；作为……的原因
vice	*n.*	an immoral or evil habit or practice; a personal shortcoming 恶行；失德行为；缺点
wickedness	*n.*	the quality of being evil or morally wrong 罪恶，邪恶，不道德

Useful Expressions

be embedded in	to become a permanent and noticeable feature of a society or system, or someone's personality 植根于；嵌入
be immune to	to confer immunity (to disease or infection); not affected by a given influence 对……有免疫力；不受影响的
be in favor of	to support sth. and think that it is good 赞成，支持

Unit 6 Cultural Values

Cultural Notes

1. Kluckhohn and Strodtbeck

Florence R. Kluckhohn (1879–1968) and Fred L. Strodtbeck (1919–2005) are both American scholars of sociology. They are famous for Kluckhohn and Strodtbeck's Values Orientation Theory which they proposed in *Variations in Value Orientations* published in 1961. They propose that all human societies must answer a limited number of universal problems that are value-based, but that different cultures have different preferences among them.

2. *Three-Character Classic*

Three-Character Classic (《三字经》) is one of the key traditional texts from Chinese culture that is believed to have been written sometime in the 13th century. The text, with the traditional name *San Zi Jing*, is also known as the *Trimetric* (三音步的) *Classic*. The text focuses on imparting Confucian teaching to children.

3. Geert H. Hofstede

Geert H. Hofstede (1928–2020) is a Dutch organizational psychologist who enjoys an international reputation in the field of intercultural studies. He is famous for his development of the Hofstede cultural dimensions during a survey study within IBM in the 1960s. This organizational culture model can help to identify cultural differences.

4. The Enlightenment

The Enlightenment (启蒙运动), also known as the Age of Enlightenment, was an intellectual and philosophical movement that dominated Europe in the 17th and 18th centuries with global influences and effects. The Enlightenment included a range of ideas centered on the value of human happiness, the pursuit of knowledge obtained by means of reason and the evidence of the senses, and ideals such as liberty, progress, toleration, fraternity (博爱), constitutional government, and separation of church and state.

Reading Comprehension

I. Choose the best options to answer the following questions or fill in the blanks.

1. According to the text, which of the following statements is true about "value orientation"?
   A. It forms the basic perspectives through which we view our actions as well as others'.
   B. It guides us on how to communicate appropriately as well as how to interpret and evaluate the behavior of others.

C. It varies from culture to culture.
D. All of the above.

2. According to Kluckhohn and Strodtbeck, _____ is/are the essential orientations that all cultures must address.
   A. human nature orientation
   B. relational orientation
   C. activity orientation
   D. all of the above

3. The word "inherently" in Paragraph 3 can be replaced with _____.
   A. accidentally   B. consistently
   C. innately   D. consequently

4. Which of the following statements is **NOT** true about "human nature orientation"?
   A. Humans are born to be either good or bad.
   B. According to Confucianism, human nature consists of sympathy, justice, respect and wisdom.
   C. Some traditions within Christianity place great emphasis on the present sinfulness and capacity for depravity in human nature.
   D. Human nature can be rather complicated in different cultural contexts.

5. According to the text, "individualism" differs from "collectivism" in a way that _____.
   A. individualism emphasizes self-concept while collectivism values the concept of group.
   B. "I" consciousness prevails in collectivist cultures while "we" consciousness is more highlighted in individualist cultures.
   C. cooperation is highly valued in individualist cultures whereas competition is encouraged in collectivist cultures.
   D. people in collectivist cultures tend to be more independent while those in individualist cultures are more interrelated and interdependent.

6. According to the text, which of the following statements is true about "anthropocosmic world view" and "anthropocentric world view"?
   A. The anthropocosmic world view envisions human individuals as the center of everything in the cosmos.
   B. From the anthropocentric world view, human is isolated from the natural world.
   C. Harmony of humans with nature is a reflection of the anthropocentric world view.

Unit 6 Cultural Values

   D. The anthropocentric world view regards nature as the center of the cosmos.

7. Which of the following descriptions might be true for Latin Americans?
   A. They emphasize schedules, segmentation and promptness.
   B. They are more rigid and clock-bound.
   C. Time for them is more flexible and more human-centered.
   D. They belong to M-time cultures.

II. **Decide whether the following statements are TRUE, FALSE, or NOT GIVEN according to the information given in the text.**

1. One of the most influential and pioneering researches about value orientation was proposed by Kluckhohn and Strodtbeck in the early 1940s.

2. Harmony of humans with nature is one of the most significant contributions Confucian tradition offers to the global community.

3. The anthropocentric world view is consistent with Confucianism.

4. The word "alienated" in Paragraph 9 probably means "isolated".

5. The Enlightenment of the 17th and 18th centuries in Europe laid the foundation for the anthropocentric view.

6. The Asian cultures prefer "doing" orientation while the Western cultures value "being" orientation.

7. According to the author, most post-industrial cultures are future-oriented.

Checking Basic Concepts

Complete the following statements with a proper word or phrase in the box. Each word or phrase can be used only once.

> activity orientation   monochronic time cultures
> anthropocentric world view   personhood
> anthropocosmic world view   polychronic time cultures
> collectivism   values
> individualism   value orientations

1. The norms that underlie cultural patterns and guide the society in response to physical and social environments are called _____.

2. The ways in which human beings in all cultures of the world deal with problems in terms of values are known as _____.

3. _____ refers to the practice or principle of placing the interests of a group over those of each individual in it.

4. A social theory favoring freedom of action for individuals over collective or state control is known as _____.

5. _____ emphasizes the harmony of humans with nature.

6. _____ envisions the human individual as the center of everything in the cosmos, and all others including nature are scaled or rated with interest, freedom, and dignity of the individual as the reference.

7. The way the people of a culture view human actions and how they express themselves through activities is known as _____.

8. The quality or condition of being an individual person is _____.

9. People in _____ perceive time as a linear structure and emphasize on schedules, segmentation and promptness.

10. In _____, time for people is more flexible and more human-centered.

Language in Use

I. Complete the following sentences with the words in the box. Change the form if necessary. Each word can be used only once.

underlie	innate	dominate	coherent
alienate	flourish	myriad	envision

1. Murphy, in his own way, has battled on to _____ in a harsh sports environment.

2. It was easy to write a report on the essay that we read since it was _____.

3. Trying to figure out what feeling _____ your anger is an effective way to control your emotion.

4. As a child he was _____ by his father.

5. Knowledge is acquired, not _____.

6. They _____ an equal society, free of poverty and disease.

7. Very talented children may feel _____ from the others in their class.

8. They face a(n) _____ of problems bringing up children.

II. Paraphrase the following sentences from Text A.

1. The harmony of humans with nature is one of the most significant contributions the Confucian tradition can offer to the building of a global community.

   _____
   _____
   _____

2. M-time is noted for its emphasis on schedules, segmentation and promptness. It features one event at a time. Time is perceived as a linear structure just like a ribbon stretching from the past into the future.

   _____
   _____
   _____

Expanding Intercultural Knowledge

Hofstede-Bond Value Dimensions

Geert H. Hofstede is a Dutch interculturalist. His value dimension is perhaps the most significant study of work-related values. It involves 116,000 respondents to a questionnaire distributed in over 40 countries and regions. The participants in the study were all managers of IBM. With a huge database, he came up with four cultural dimensions on which cultures differ. His student, M. H. Bond, conducted a smaller survey later and proposed the fifth cultural dimension, thus forming Hofstede-Bond Value Dimensions.

(1) Individualism vs. Collectivism

This dimension has been used in Text A in analyzing Kluckhohn and Strodtbeck's relational orientation. In brief, it focuses on the relationship between the individual and larger social groups. As mentioned earlier, cultures vary on the amount of emphasis they place on encouraging individuality uniqueness or on conformity and interdependence.

Highly individualist cultures believe the individual is the most important unit. Highly collectivist cultures believe the group is the most important unit. According to Hofstede's study of IBM, the U.S.A. ranked number 1 in individualism worldwide, followed by Australia, Great Britain, Canada, and the Netherlands. Countries like Indonesia, South Korea, Pakistan and Peru value collectivism more.

(2) Power Distance

Power distance indicates the extent to which a society accepts the fact that power in institutions and organizations is distributed unequally among individuals.

Countries such as the U.S.A., Great Britain, Canada, Australia, New Zealand, Israel, Sweden and Switzerland are cultures with low power distance. In those cultures, power is shared and widely dispersed, and society members do not accept situations where power is distributed unequally. In management, decision-making in the workplace is decentralized (分散的); employees can participate in the decision-making process. On the contrary, countries like China, Indonesia, Malaysia, Philippines, Mexico, most Arab countries and India are cultures with high power distance. These cultures accept an unequal, hierarchical (等级的) distribution of power, and the people understand "their place" in the system. It is desirable for children to obey their parents and teachers; employees execute their managers' decisions.

(3) Uncertainty Avoidance

Uncertainty avoidance indicates the extent to which a society feels threatened by ambiguous (模糊的) situations and tries to avoid them by providing rules, believing in absolute truths, and refusing to tolerate deviance (偏离常规).

In societies that score highly for uncertainty avoidance, people attempt to make life as predictable and controllable as possible. People in low uncertainty avoidance countries tend to be more relaxed, open and inclusive. Japan, France and South Korea have high rankings in uncertainty avoidance. Countries which rank low include Singapore, China, Great Britain, Malaysia, India and the U.S.A.

(4) Masculinity vs. Femininity

This refers to the distribution of roles between men and women. "Masculinity" comes from "masculine" and implies aggressiveness and assertiveness, while "femininity" comes from "feminine" and stresses nurturing (养育) and pays attention to people's feelings and needs. In a society with a high masculinity score, such as Japan, Austria, Italy, Switzerland, Mexico, Great Britain and Germany, men dominate in society and gender differences are clear. By contrast, in a society with a low masculinity score, such as Norway, Netherlands, Denmark, Finland, Chile, Portugal, and Thailand, gender roles are more flexible, and there is equality between sexes. Quality of life has a high priority. One works in order to live. In their work, they pursue good working relationships, cooperation and employment security rather than being controlled by a dominant and assertive figure.

(5) Long-term vs. Short-term Orientation

Bond, Hofstede's student, conducted a Chinese Value Survey (CVS) later. The scope of Bond's study was much smaller, involving a survey of 100 (50% women) students from 22 countries and 5 continents. Bond's study isolated a new cultural dimension—"long-term vs. short-term orientation"—to reflect how strongly a person believes in the long-term thinking promoted by the teachings of the Chinese philosopher Confucius. Values like thrifty, persistence and saving for the future are promoted in the long-term orientation. In contrast, people with short-term orientation tend to expect quick results and immediate gratification (满足) for their needs, and spend for the present. China and India rank high in long-term orientation, whereas some European countries such as Norway, Sweden, Germany, and Belgium tend to be more short-term oriented.

As you move through these dimensions in the Hofstede-Bond Research, you will notice some of the same characteristics discussed by Kluckhohn and Strodtbeck. This is very understandable because both approaches are focused on meaningful values found in all cultures.

(Source: Dou Weilin, *Introduction to Intercultural Communication*)

Reflecting and Discussing

Compare and contrast Kluckhohn & Strodtbeck's model of cultural value orientations and Hofstede's cultural value orientations. Which model do you think is more powerful in distinguishing our Chinese culture from other cultures, and why?

Text B: Eastern vs. Western Parenting

Read Text B and do the exercises online.

Unit 6 Cultural Values

Case Study

Discuss with your classmates the questions according to each case.

Why Were They Late for Class?

John Rohrkemper was an American professor. It was his first time to teach in a Brazilian university and he was quite excited about it. His two-hour class was scheduled to begin at 10 am and end at noon. On the first day, to his surprise, there was no one in the classroom when he arrived on time. Many students came after 10 am; several arrived after 10:30 am; two students came after 11 am. Although all the students greeted him as they arrived, few apologized for their lateness. Dr. Rohrkemper was very angry about students' rude behavior and decided to study their behavior.

(Source: Chang Junyue et al., *Intercultural Communication*)

1. What do you think Dr. Rohrkemper will find in his study about Brazilian students' lateness?

2. What suggestions would you like to give to both Dr. Rohrkemper and his Brazilian students?

An Intercultural Classroom

It was a hot day. Since it was still too early to use the air-conditioner, according to the regulations of the university, every class kept its door open to make the classroom cooler. While I was lecturing on Chinese grammar in Class 4, waves of laughter came from the neighboring Class 5.

A German student named Stephen raised his hand and stood up. "The laughter from Class 5 is bothering us. I think we should go to their class to protest," he said.

His deskmate, a student from Japan, shook his head. "Is it necessary to protest over such a minor issue? I can tolerate this noise. And there are some

Japanese friends of mine in Class 5. I don't want to make my friends unhappy just because of their laughter."

Another Japanese girl stood up, "Let me close our door. Although that will make it hotter, it will be quieter."

She was stopped by a French student. "Why should we close our door and suffer from the heat? Class 5 should close their door in order not to bother other classes."

A few students from Africa suggested, "Why not strike our desks like drums to protest?"

A girl from Russia agreed, "Our class could also laugh together to let them know what the noise sounds like."

Two Korean students whispered to each other, "Western students really have a hot temper. They just don't know how to stay calm. How could we get along well with other classes if we can't control ourselves?"

A Hungarian (匈牙利的) girl happened to overhear their comments. She disagreed, "I don't understand you Asians. You won't protest even when your rights have been violated."

More laughter came from Class 5. Stephen stood up, "No matter what you think about it, I'm going to protest." He went to Class 5 and asked, "How happy you must be today! May we share with your happiness?" Laughter stopped. After a while, Class 5 closed their door.

Stephen came back satisfied and told his Japanese classmates, "Now you Asians can enjoy the peace won by us Westerners." When the class was over, a few European students from Class 5 came to apologize to me. They weren't aware that their happy laughter might have bothered Class 4. The Japanese students from Class 5, however, took Stephen as being "斤斤计较" (people who are aggressive over trifles).

(Source: Fan Weiwei, *A Multimedia Approach to Intercultural Communication*)

1. How many different solutions did Class 4 propose to the noise coming from Class 5?

2. What did the European students insist on doing and why?

3. What did the Asian students prefer to do?

4. What different cultural values underlie their preference?

Unit 7
Language and Culture

To have another language is to possess a second soul.

—*Charlemagne*

三寸之舌，强于百万雄兵。

——《战国策》

Learning Objectives

Upon completion of this unit, you will be able to:

- Define the concept of *language*.
- Explain the functions of language.
- Understand how language is closely related to culture.
- Analyze the denotative and connotative meanings of words.
- Compare and contrast different verbal styles.
- Understand variations of human language.

 Lead-in

Eastern vs. Western Verbal Styles

Study the following two versions of the same spoken discourse presented at a business meeting by a Chinese businessman and an American businessman. Decide in small groups which one might have been given by a Chinese and which one by an American, and what is the reasoning behind your decision.

A. Although most of our production is done in China now, it's not really clear how things will be like in the coming years, and uh, I think a certain amount of caution in committing to TV advertisement is necessary due to the great expense. So I suggest that we delay making our decision.

B. I suggest that we delay making our decision. That's because I think a certain amount of caution in committing to TV advertisement is necessary due to the great expense. In addition to that, although most of our production is done in China now, it's not really clear how things will be like in the coming years.

(Source: Wang Rong & Zhang Ailin, *Bridge Between Minds: Intercultural Communication*)

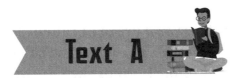

The Connection Between Language and Culture

1   *Language*, to put it most simply, is a set of codes and symbols, along with the rules for combining them together. People in different cultures have different codes, symbols and rules to facilitate their communication. For example, Chinese people use "花", while British people use "flower" to **designate** the same thing.

2   Everyone makes daily use of language in talking with friends, listening to a lecture, using a cell phone, writing a report, etc. Language also serves important communicative functions **other than** directly expressing and exchanging ideas and thoughts with others. A common language allows individuals to form social groups and engage in cooperative efforts as in recording and preserving past events, thus, language plays an important role in the formation and expression of our identity, particularly national identity.

The Relationship Between Language and Culture

3   The language we use and the culture in which we live are closely related. Some compare language and culture to a living organism: language is flesh, and culture is blood. Without culture, language would be dead; without language, culture would have no shape. In other words, they cannot be separated and exist alone. But, which one is the stronger?

A. Language Determines Our Culture

4   Some scholars argue that language not only transmits but also shapes our thinking, beliefs, and attitudes. They say the language people speak determines the way they perceive the world, so it determines culture. That is *Language Determinism*. One form of language determinism is the *Sapir-Whorf Hypothesis*[1], proposed by two American linguists in the early years of the last century. According to Sapir, language is the medium of expression for human society, and it conditions our thinking about social problems and processes.

B. Language Reflects Our Attitude

5   However, other scholars argue that language merely reflects, rather than shapes our thinking, beliefs, and attitudes. They claim that language reflects the degree of power one can **wield**. They cite as examples the following expressions

of powerless language: "I guess I'd like to..." "I think I should..." "Well, we could try this idea..." "I'm not really sure, but..." and so on. The degree of intimacy with people is reflected through words such as "baby" "buddy" and "dear"; willingness to take or not take responsibility is reflected through the use of "it" "we" "you" and "but" statements. Thus, every culture, by means of its own language system, expresses universal human feelings and attitudes.

Denotation and Connotation

6   Culture has an impact on language at various levels. The word is the basic element of a language and it reveals the corresponding culture. The meaning of words can largely be grouped into two types: ***denotation*** and ***connotation***. Denotation is the conceptual meaning of a word that designates or describes things, events or processes, etc. It is the primary, explicit meaning given in the definition of a word in a dictionary. Connotation refers to the emotional or **figurative** associations that a word or phrase suggests in one's mind. It is the **implicit**, **supplementary** value which is added to the purely denotative meaning of a word or phrase.

A. Cultural Differences in Denotative Meaning

7   Each culture creates certain vocabulary to describe its unique physical and social environments as well as the activities its people engage in. Words like "炕" "节气" "关系" "德育" and "三纲五常" can only make sense to the Chinese, and words like "Thanksgiving Day" and "parliament" are foreign to the Chinese. Cultures also **overlap** in the denotation of certain vocabulary. For example, the languages of the Chinese, British and Eskimos[2] all have words that refer to the natural phenomenon "snow", but the Chinese and English languages only have a general term for this while the Eskimos have many words for different kinds of snow. So the meaning of the word "snow" in English or Chinese language does not **coincide** with the meanings expressed by the Eskimos' words, which are more specific and **minute**. The implication for intercultural communicators is that they must learn or use the words in another language with the right denotation. Otherwise, their communication will be based on wrong references and misunderstandings will follow up.

B. Cultural Differences in Connotative Meaning

8   A typical example of this kind of distinction is the color language. The Chinese and English both have words denoting the basic colors, but the meanings associated with these color words are quite different. For example,

"yellow" in English is usually associated with the state of being **cowardly**, as in "yellow-bellied". In Chinese, however, the word "黄色" carries the meaning of being **pornographic** and **obscene**, as in "黄色书刊" "黄色电影". Not knowing such differences, people may translate such Chinese terms directly into English as "yellow books" and "yellow movies", which seems **bizarre** or ridiculous to English speakers.

9 Animal words may also have different connotations in different languages. The Chinese "dragon" is the **totem** of the Chinese people. Its common associations are "good luck and fortune" "royal and noble" etc. There are many phrases to show Chinese people's love for this legendary animal: "龙凤呈祥" "藏龙卧虎" "龙头企业", etc. In English, the word "dragon" refers to a **dreadful** creature like a crocodile or snake, and it is associated with fierceness and has a **derogatory** sense when used to describe a person.

10 Numbers, due to their sounds or stories about them, may also have special meanings in certain cultures. "13" is the most unwelcome number in Western countries. "4" is to be avoided in China, Japan and South Korea for its similar sound with the word "death" or "to die" in these languages. "8" is loved by many Chinese as it sounds like "发" in Cantonese, meaning "to be prosperous".

Verbal Communication Styles

11 Culture's influence on language is also reflected in different verbal styles. Edward Hall distinguishes among cultures on the basis of the role of context in communication. Hall categorizes cultures as being either high-context or low-context.

12 In *high-context cultures* (HCC), such as those of Japan, Korea and China, most of the information is in the physical context, and very little information is actually coded in the verbal message. The listener is expected to "read between the lines". In *low-context cultures* (LCC), such as those of Germany and America, however, most of the information is contained in the verbal message, and very little is embedded in the context. The speaker is expected to "say what you mean, and mean what you say".

A. Direct and Indirect Verbal Styles

13 People's verbal styles depend on their identities, intentions, interaction goals, relationship types, and the situation. However, in individualistic cultures, people tend to encounter more situations that emphasize a direct style. In contrast, in collectivistic cultures, people tend to encounter more situations that emphasize

the use of indirect style.

14   The direct and indirect styles differ in how they reveal the speaker's intentions through tone of voice and the straightforwardness of the content in the message. *The direct style* emphasizes that the statements reveal the speaker's intentions with clarity and are expressed with a **forthright** tone of voice. *The indirect style*, on the other hand, emphasizes that the statements **camouflage** the speaker's actual intentions and are carried out with a softer tone. For example, while Americans tend to use a straightforward form of communication in a request situation, Koreans tend to ask for a favor in a more **roundabout** and implicit way so as not to sound so **imposing** or **demanding**.

B. Self-Enhancement and Self-Humbling Verbal Styles

15   Another verbal pattern is the **spectrum** between self-**enhancement** and self-**humbling** verbal style. *The self-enhancement style* emphasizes the importance of drawing attention to or exaggerating one's outstanding accomplishments, and special abilities. *The self-humbling style*, on the other hand, emphasizes the importance of **downplaying** oneself via modest talk, restraint, hesitation, and the use of self-**deprecation** messages concerning one's performance or effort. In Swiss or American culture, individuals are encouraged to "sell themselves and boast about their achievements". However, the notion of **merchandising** oneself does not **sit well with** many Latin Americans and Asians.

16   Overall, LCC like the United States, Australia, Canada, Germany and Switzerland emphasizes a direct and self-enhancement verbal style. In comparison, HCC like Japan, China, Brazil, the Middle East and Latin America stresses an indirect and self-humbling verbal style.

(Source: Guo-Ming Chen & William J. Starosta, *Foundations of Intercultural Communication*, Chapter 4; Chang Junyue et al., *Intercultural Communication*, Unit 3; Stella Ting-Toomey & Leeva C. Chung, *Understanding Intercultural Communication*, Chapter 6)

New Words

bizarre	*adj.*	very strange and unusual 奇怪的，古怪的
camouflage	*v.*	to hide sb./sth. by making them look like the things around, or like sth. else 伪装；掩饰
coincide	*v.*	to be the same or very similar 相同，相符，极为类似

connotation	n.	an idea suggested by a word in addition to its main meaning 隐含意义
cowardly	adj.	easily frightened and avoid doing dangerous and difficult things 胆小的，怯懦的
demanding	adj.	needing a lot of skill, patience, effort, etc. 要求高的；需要高技能或耐心等的；费力的
denotation	n.	the act of naming sth. with a word; the actual object or idea to which the word refers 指称；指称之物；指称意义；外延
deprecation	n.	the action of saying that you think sth. is of little value or importance 贬低
derogatory	adj.	showing a critical or disrespectful attitude towards sb./sth. 贬低的；贬义的
designate	v.	to say officially that sth. has a particular character or name; to describe sth. in a particular way 命名，指定
downplay	v.	to make people think that sth. is less important than it really is 对……轻描淡写；使轻视，贬低
dreadful	adj.	disagreeable, shocking, or bad; causing dread; terrifying 糟糕的；讨厌的；可怕的
enhancement	n.	the improvement of sb./sth. in relation to the value, quality, or attractiveness 提升；美化
figurative	adj.	(of words and phrases) used not with their basic meaning but with a more imaginative meaning in order to create a special effect 比喻性的，象征性的
forthright	adj.	direct and honest in manner and speech 直率的，直截了当的
humble	adj.	showing you do not think that you are as important as other people 谦逊的，虚心的
implicit	adj.	suggested; without being directly expressed 含蓄的，不直接言明的

imposing	adj.	pushing others too hard or making them accept one's idea, opinion, etc. 强迫的，强加的
merchandise	v.	to sell sth. using advertising, etc. 推销，（运用广告等）销售
minute	adj.	very detailed, careful and thorough 细致入微的，详细的
obscene	adj.	connected with sex in a way that most people find offensive 淫秽的，猥亵的，下流的
overlap	v.	to lie or extend over and cover part of sth. （物体）部分重叠，交叠
pornographic	adj.	intended to make people feel sexually excited by showing naked people or sexual acts, usually in a way that many other people find offensive 下流的，黄色的，色情的
roundabout	adj.	not done or said using the shortest, simplest or most direct way possible 迂回的，间接的，兜圈子的
spectrum	n.	a complete or wide range of related qualities, ideas, etc. 范围；层次；系列；幅度
supplementary	adj.	provided in addition to sth. else in order to improve or complete it 增补性的，补充性的，额外的，外加的
totem	n.	an animal or other natural object that is chosen and respected as a special symbol of a community or family, especially among Native Americans; an image of this animal, etc. （尤指美洲土著的）图腾，图腾形象
wield	v.	to have and use power, authority, etc. 拥有，运用，行使，支配（权力等）

Useful Expressions

other than	except for; besides 除……之外
sit well with	to be agreeable to one's values or sensibilities （观点，观念等）受欢迎

Unit 7 Language and Culture

Cultural Notes

1. Sapir-Whorf Hypothesis

Sapir-Whorf hypothesis (萨皮尔－沃尔夫假说) is the linguistic theory that the semantic structure of a language shapes or limits the ways in which a speaker forms conceptions of the world. It was first proposed in 1929. The theory is named after the American anthropological linguist Edward Sapir (1884–1939) and his student Benjamin Whorf (1897–1941). It is also known as the theory of linguistic relativity (语言相对论).

2. Eskimos

Eskimos (爱斯基摩人) refer to two closely related indigenous peoples: the Inuit (因纽特人) and the Yupik (尤皮克人) of eastern Siberia (西伯利亚) and Alaska (阿拉斯加). A related third group, the Aleut (阿留申岛人), who inhabit the Aleutian Islands, are generally excluded from the definition of Eskimo. The three groups share a relatively recent common ancestor, and speak related languages belonging to the Eskimo-Aleut language family.

Reading Comprehension

I. Choose the best options to answer the following questions or fill in the blanks.

1. What is mainly talked about in the text?
   A. Definition of language.
   B. The relation between language and culture.
   C. Denotative and connotative meanings of words.
   D. High-context and low-context cultures.

2. The functions of language include _____.
   A. social interaction
   B. expression of ideas and thoughts
   C. expression of identity
   D. all of the above

3. "Sapir-Whorf Hypothesis", when applied to communication in general, states that _____.
   A. people use silence to reflect situations of uncertainty
   B. people use different language in different social situations
   C. language reflects people's view of the world
   D. language shapes people's view of the world

4. "Denotation" refers to _____.
   A. the figurative meaning of a word
   B. the suggested meaning of a word
   C. the set of associations implied by a word
   D. the most specific and direct meaning of a word

5. Many words from Chinese and English are different in both the denotative and connotative meanings. Which of the following is an example of this?
   A. 鸽子/dove   B. 猫头鹰/owl
   C. 龙/dragon   D. 红/red

6. According to the text, which of the following statements is **NOT** true?
   A. Direct styles are often used in low-context, individualistic cultures.
   B. The use of ambiguity and vagueness is characteristic of an indirect style.
   C. In Swiss culture, people are encouraged to use self-enhancement verbal style.
   D. In American culture, people tend to use self-humbling verbal style.

7. All of the following countries belong to HCC **EXCEPT** _____.
   A. the U.S.A.   B. China   C. Japan   D. Brazil

II. Decide whether the following statements are TRUE, FALSE, or NOT GIVEN according to the information given in the text.

1. There are as many similarities as dissimilarities between English and Chinese.

   _____

2. Connotation is the conceptual meaning of the word that designates or describes things, events, processes, etc.

   _____

3. Each culture creates a certain vocabulary to describe its unique physical and social environments as well as the activities its people engage in.

   _____

4. A term in one language may not have a counterpart (对应物) in another language.

   _____

5. The meaning of the word "snow" in English or Chinese coincides with the meanings expressed by the Eskimos' words.

   _____

6. Misunderstandings will arise when intercultural communicators don't use the words in another language with the right denotation.

   _____

7. Verbal style is more important than meanings of words in intercultural communication.

   _____

Checking Basic Concepts

Complete the following statements with a proper word or phrase in the box. Each word or phrase can be used only once.

connotation	language
denotation	language determinism
direct verbal style	low-context cultures
high-context cultures	self-enhancement style
indirect verbal style	self-humbling verbal style

1. To put it most simply, _____ is a set of codes and symbols, along with the rules for combining them together.

2. The theory that language shapes our thinking, beliefs, and attitudes is known as _____.

3. The primary, explicit meaning given in the definition of a word in a dictionary is called the word's _____.

4. _____ refers to the emotional or stylistic associations that a word or phrase suggests in one's mind.

5. In _____, most of the information is in the physical context, and very little information is actually coded in the verbal message.

6. Cultures in which most of the information is contained in the verbal message, and very little is embedded in the context are known as _____.

7. In _____, statements tend to reveal the speaker's intentions with clarity and are expressed with a forthright tone of voice.

8. In _____, when people need to ask for a favor, they tend to do it in a more roundabout and implicit way to sound not so imposing or demanding.

9. The verbal style that emphasizes the importance of drawing attention to or exaggerating one's outstanding accomplishments and special abilities is known as _____.

10. _____ emphasizes the importance of downplaying oneself via modest talk, restraint, hesitation, and the use of self-deprecation message concerning one's performance or effort.

Language in Use

I. **Complete the following sentences with the words in the box. Change the form if necessary. Each word can be used only once.**

demanding	cowardly	humble	merchandise
designate	dreadful	downplay	coincide

1. There are efforts underway to _____ the bridge a historic landmark.

2. I was too _____ to complain.

3. The interests of employers and employees do not always _____.

4. We've made a(n) _____ mistake.

5. He gave a great performance, but he was very _____.

6. He tried to return to work, but found he could no longer cope with his _____ job.

7. It is irresponsible for the government officials to _____ the severity of the crisis and assure the public that everything is under control.

8. In hope that the business would recover from deficit, the company decides to _____ their goods to attract more consumers.

Unit 7 Language and Culture

II. Paraphrase the following sentences from Text A.

1. Everyone makes daily use of language in talking with friends, listening to a lecture, using a cell phone, writing a report, etc. Language also serves important communicative functions other than directly expressing and exchanging ideas and thoughts with others.

_____

_____

_____

2. However, other scholars argue that language merely reflects, rather than shapes our thinking, beliefs, and attitudes.

_____

_____

_____

 # Expanding Intercultural Knowledge

Variations of Human Language

In addition to what is discussed in Text A, cultures are also characterized by a number of internal linguistic variations. These differences are usually culturally influenced and frequently offer hints as to the nation or region where a person lives or grew up, his/her age, level of education, and socioeconomic status.

Accent

Accents are simply variations in pronunciation that occur when people are speaking the same language. These are often a result of geographical or historical differences, such as those among English speakers in Australia, Canada, England, South Africa, and the United States. In the United States, you often hear regional accents characterized as "Southern" "New England" or "New York".

Dialect

Dialects reflect regional differences in vocabulary, grammar, and even pronunciation. Chinese is usually considered to have eight distinct, major dialects (Cantonese, Hakka, etc.), which are bound by a common writing system but are mutually unintelligible when spoken. English spoken in the United States is characterized by a number of dialects. For example, Black English Vernacular (非洲裔美国人白话英语) represents a very distinct dialect in the United States.

Lingua Franca

When a given language known to all the participants is used by common agreement for the purpose of communication, this language is called lingua franca. Hindustani (印度斯坦语), Hindi (北印度语), Urdu (乌尔都语), Persian (波斯语), and Punjabi (印度旁遮普地区语言) are used as lingua franca in India. Swahili (斯瓦希里语) is used as a lingua franca in Africa to conduct business. Yiddish (意第绪语) can be considered a lingua franca that is used by Jewish people to bind them together. Moreover, English has been called the lingua franca of the whole world, because it is the first or second language for 54 percent of the business world and is used by most international airlines.

Jargon

Jargon refers to the special or technical vocabularies developed to meet the special needs of particular professions. For example, "CD-ROM" "megabyte" and "default" (默认值) are jargon in the computer field. A communication major may understand the terms "coding" and "feedback" better than others. And, unless we are pilots, we might not understand the real meaning of "touch-and-go" (连续起飞).

Taboo

All cultures have taboos related to the use of language. These can be cultural restrictions against discussing a topic in a particular setting, or prohibitions against using certain words. A culture's verbal taboos generally relate to sex, the supernatural, excretion (排泄行为), and death, but quite often they extend to other aspects of domestic and social life. For example, in Saudi Arabia, asking about a person's family can cause considerable offense. In the United States, we are taught that it is impolite to ask a person's age, sexual orientation, or religion, and to refrain from arguing about politics. However, in many European nations, vigorous debates about political activities are quite acceptable.

Euphemism

The word "euphemism" (委婉语) comes from Greek: "eu" meaning "good" and "pheme" meaning "speech". They are frequently employed in everyday language and literature to replace words that some people deem offensive.

English and Chinese have certain areas of agreement on euphemisms. For example, when talking about death, Chinese often use "逝世" "辞世" "走了" "没了", etc. In English, euphemisms of death include "pass away" "go to heaven" "depart" and so on. In Chinese, people use "去洗手间" "解手" "去方便一下" instead of "上厕所". "Wash one's hands" "pay a call" "powder one's face" and "relieve oneself" are euphemisms of going to the toilet in English. "有了" "有喜" and "be in a family way" "be expecting" "be a mother-to-be" are roundabout expressions of being pregnant. "发福" "富态" and "putting on weight" are euphemisms of "being fat". "城市美容师" and "sanitation engineer" actually mean "garbage man". "长者" "前辈" and "senior citizens" "grey-headed" refer to old people. "学困生" "underachievers" and "students with untapped (未被开发的) potential" are euphemistic expressions of poor or lazy students.

(Source: Larry A. Samovar et al., *Communication Between Cultures* and Guo-Ming Chen & William J. Starosta, *Foundations of Intercultural Communication*)

Reflecting and Discussing

1. Do you know any technical jargon in your area of study?
2. Do you know any other taboos and euphemisms in Chinese and other languages?

How Language Shapes the Way We Think

Read Text B and do the exercises online.

Case Study

Discuss with your classmates the questions according to each case.

 Case 1

Look Out!

A foreign student in the U.S. was sitting by a window reading a book. She heard someone yelling "Look out!" So she stuck her head out of the window. Just then a board hurtled (猛冲) down from above, narrowly missing her. She looked up, half in anger and half in fright. There was a man on the roof doing repairs. "Didn't you hear me call 'Look out'?" he demanded. "Yes, and that's what I did." she replied.

(Source: Hu Chao, *Intercultural Communication: A Practical Coursebook*)

In this case, what does "look out" mean? Could you give a similar case like this?

 Case 2

Conversations Between Neighbors

Scene 1 and Scene 2 are conversations between neighbors under the same situation.

Scene 1 (Two European American neighbors)

Jane (knocks on her neighbor's open window): Excuse me, it is 11 o'clock already, and your high-pitched opera singing is really disturbing my sleep. Please stop your gargling (漱口声似的) noises immediately! I have an important job interview tomorrow morning, and I want to get a good night's sleep. I really need this job to pay my rent!

Diane (resentfully): Well, this is the only time I can rehearse my opera! I have an important audition (试镜) coming up tomorrow. You're not the only one that is starving, you know. I also need to pay my rent. Stop being so self-centered!

Jane (frustrated): I really think you're being very unreasonable. If you don't stop your singing right now, I'm going to file a complaint with the apartment manager and he could evict (驱逐) you...

Diane (sarcastically 嘲讽地): OK, be my guest (请便)... Do whatever you want. I'm going to sing as I please.

Scene 2 (Two Japanese housewives)

Mrs. A: Your daughter has started taking piano lessons, hasn't she? I envy you, because you can be proud of her talent. You must be looking forward to her future as a pianist. I'm really impressed by her enthusiasm, every day, she practices so hard, for hours and hours, until late at night.

Mrs. B: Oh, no, not at all. She's just a beginner. We don't know her future yet. We hadn't realized that you could hear her playing. I'm so sorry you have been disturbed by her noise.

(Source: Anna Trosborg, *Pragmatics Across Languages and Cultures*)

1. Why are there different results from the two scenes?

2. What verbal styles are used by the speakers in Scene 1 and Scene 2? What are the features of these styles?

3. Which verbal style do you prefer? Why?

Unit 8

Nonverbal Communication and Culture

There's language in her eye, her cheek, her lip; Nay, her foot speaks.
—William Shakespeare

知者不言，言者不知。
——《道德经》

Learning Objectives

Upon completion of this unit, you will be able to:

- Define the concept of *nonverbal communication*.
- Explain the main functions of nonverbal communication.
- Know the main areas of study in nonverbal communication.
- Understand the impact of culture on nonverbal communication.
- Compare and contrast body language in different cultures.
- Understand different personal space across cultures.

Lead-in

Obama's Bow in Japan

The U.S. former President Obama went on a week-long tour in Asia in 2009. While visiting Japan, he met Japanese Emperor Akihito and Empress Michiko. In the meeting, he shook hands with the Emperor with a low bow. However, this seemingly innocent physical behavior erupted into (引发) a hot controversy that was traveling the Internet and news outlet (新闻媒体) for days. People from different cultures were either outraged (气愤的) at Obama's action, or they saw the bow as a sign of respect. Some critics stated that the President should stand tall when representing America overseas.

(Source: Jia Yuxin, *Experiencing Global Intercultural Communication*)

Questions for Intercultural Understanding

1. Collect all the information relevant to Obama's bowing and the reactions to it from different cultures. Give your viewpoint and reasons behind it.

2. Figure out what bow and other relevant behavior really mean in Japan, the U.S.A. and other cultures involved.

Unit 8 Nonverbal Communication and Culture

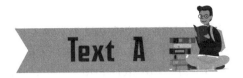

The Silent Language

1   If anyone asks you about the main means of communication between people, what would you say? The answer would certainly involve the use of words. You would be quite right. There is, however, another form of communication which we all use most of the time, usually without knowing it. This is called nonverbal communication.

2   According to Edward T. Hall, *nonverbal communication* is the silent language, and the hidden dimension of communication. We may simply say that nonverbal communication is communication without the use of words.

Importance of Nonverbal Communication

3   Researchers have shown that the words a person speaks may be far less important than the body language used when delivering messages. They estimate that less than 35% of communication between two individuals within the same culture is verbal. 65% of communication then takes place nonverbally. Researchers also indicate that sometimes nonverbal signals play a more decisive role than verbal messages in determining communicative effects. For instance, whether what you say is a joke or an insult depends on the facial expression and tone that accompany what you say. Sometimes, it's often not what you say that **counts** but what you don't say.

4   Nonverbal communication is important to the study of intercultural communication because a lack of knowledge of another culture's nonverbal communication patterns may cause serious cultural conflicts.

Functions of Nonverbal Communication

5   Different nonverbal behavior serve different functions and exist in different relationships to verbal communication. Nonverbal behavior can accomplish several tasks. These include showing our attitudes, marking our identities, managing turn-taking in conversation, and releasing emotional tension, etc. Culture can differ on several of these dimensions.

6   Nonverbal behavior also works together with verbal communication. Nonverbal behavior can clarify what the verbal behavior conveys, or they can **contradict** each other—as happens in **sarcasm**. Head nods, eye contact, **intonation**, and

body **posture** may have different meanings across cultures. For example, a head nod or "mm hmm" in one culture might mean "I am paying attention", but in another culture it might mean "I understand what you are saying".

Classification of Nonverbal Communication

7   In broad terms, nonverbal communication covers four areas: time language (temporal language or **chronemics**), space language (spatial language or **proxemics**), body language (body movement or **kinesics**), and **paralanguage** (voice **modulation**).

8   *Chronemics* is the study of how we use time in communication. The core of it, time orientation, has been discussed in Unit 6. *Proxemics*, including the study of body distance and body touch, will be discussed in Text B. This text will focus on kinesics and paralanguage.

A. Kinesics

9   *Kinesics* or body language means more than just hand or arm gestures. It refers to any little movement of any part of the body. Generally speaking, it includes posture, gesture, facial expression, eye contact, etc.

(1) Posture

10 *Posture*, the way people hold their bodies when they sit, stand or walk, can send positive or negative nonverbal messages. When people are interacting in an intercultural environment, sharp differences can be seen in terms of what postures are taken and what meanings they convey.

11 When it comes to standing, Northern Europeans consider **slouching** very impolite. Thus, if you slouch in front of a Northern European, it can be regarded as very disrespectful. When it comes to sitting, Japanese have a strict rule. They prefer to sit on their legs, so if you sit with your legs crossed in a very traditional Japanese family, you may have the chance to offend the hosts. When it comes to bowing, Asians usually do it more frequently than Westerners. Obama bowed to heads of state in China and Japan while visiting the two countries to show respect for Asian culture. For typical North Americans, **squatting** seems improper or **uncivilized**. But Chinese farmers in the northwestern regions have developed the squatting posture, which is so strong a habit that it is still retained years after these people move to cities or the South. Squatting is also a common posture of rural Mexicans.

Unit 8 Nonverbal Communication and Culture

(2) Gesture

12 *Gestures* are another aspect of body language. Gestures can be **emblems** or symbols ("V" for victory), illustrators (police officer's hand held up to stop traffic), regulators (glancing at your watch to signal that you are in a hurry), or affection displays (one's face turns red with embarrassment). Gesture, like any other form of body language, is culture-specific. Some gestures, such as thumbs-up, thumbs-down, OK, and "V" signs, are more widely used than others. A perfectly proper gesture in one country may be considered rude in another. For example, the "V" sign is a signal for victory in the United States and many other countries. It also signals the number "two" in China. But in England and South Africa, it has a rude connotation when used with the palm in, i.e., the "V" sign done with your palm facing yourself and **thrust** upward.

(3) Facial Expressions

13 How, when and to whom facial expressions are displayed is often **dictated** by cultural norms. In many Mediterranean cultures, people exaggerate signs of grief or sadness. It is quite common to see men crying in public in this region. Yet in the United States, males often suppress these emotions. Japanese men even go so far as to hide expressions of anger, sorrow, or disappointment by laughing or smiling. Chinese also do not readily show emotion for the reason that is rooted deeply in the Chinese concept of "saving face".

(4) Eye Contact

14 Eyes speak in interpersonal communication. Cross-culturally, the misinterpretation of the use of eye contact can lead to serious misunderstanding. In North American and Northern European cultures, eye contact shows openness, trustworthiness, and **integrity**. However, staring at someone while talking is impolite in many Asian countries and the Middle East. A person from Japan, for example, would feel uncomfortable with intense eye contact. In Muslim countries, women and men are not supposed to have eye contact. But Italian men may gaze at women all the time and the women don't feel offended.

15 Direct eye contact is a taboo or an insult in many Asian cultures. Cambodians (柬埔寨人) consider direct eye contact as an invasion of one's privacy. In ancient China, looking straight into the eyes of elders will be taken as being impolite. But that changes over time. Now Chinese consider such gazing as attentive listening.

B. Paralanguage

16 *Paralanguage* refers to the study of voice or the use of vocal signs in communication. It includes **nonphonemic** properties of speech, such as speaking **tempo**, vocal **pitch**, and intonation.

17 Voice modulation carries very strong emotional **overtones**. It is said that the English word "yes" can be **uttered** in more than fifty different ways to show different emotions, attitudes and meanings. The same is true with its Chinese counterpart "好". People's vocal pitch, tempo, volume and intonation not only serve as an emotional indication but also illustrate cultural variation.

18 Silence is another element that indicates cultural **divergence**. It is interpreted as evidence of **passivity**, ignorance, or hesitation in American culture. Americans fail to appreciate Japanese speech habits, which view silence as necessary and desirable. They tend to think that there is no communication in silence and try to fill in the pauses in conversation, which unfortunately can be misunderstood as **pushy** and noisy. To Japanese, silence is a rich communication style and they regard it as a virtue.

19 Nonverbal communication and verbal communication are **inextricably** interconnected. Reading postures, gestures, facial expressions, eye contact and vocal signs help to increase our sensitivity to the **intricacies** of intercultural communication. To really know another culture, we must first learn the verbal language, and then we must be able to hear the silent language and read the invisible messages.

(Source: Dou Weilin, *Introduction to Intercultural Communication*, Chapter 5 and Hu Chao, *Intercultural Communication: A Practical Coursebook*, Unit 5)

New Words

chronemics	n.	the study of the use of time in nonverbal communication 时间学
contradict	v.	to be so different from each other that one of them must be wrong 相抵触，相矛盾，相反
count	v.	to be important; to matter 重要
dictate	v.	to control or influence how sth. happens 支配，摆布，决定

Unit 8 Nonverbal Communication and Culture

divergence	n.	drawing apart (as of lines extending from a common center); difference, disagreement 分离；分歧
emblem	n.	sth. that represents a perfect example or a principle 象征，标志
inextricably	adv.	in a way that is impossible to separate 不可分开地，密不可分地
integrity	n.	the quality of being honest and having strong moral principles 诚实，正直
intonation	n.	the rise and fall of the voice in speaking, especially as this affects the meaning of what is being said 语调
intricacy	n.	the complicatedness of sth. 复杂（的事物）
kinesics	n.	the study of the role of body movements, such as winking, shrugging, etc. in communication 人体动作学
modulation	n.	an inflection of the tone or pitch of the voice, specifically the use of stress or pitch to convey meaning（声音）调整；调节
nonphonemic	adj.	not relating to the phonemes of a language 非音素的；无辨义作用的
overtone	n.	an attitude or emotion that is suggested and is not expressed in a direct way 弦外之音，言外之意，暗示
paralanguage	n.	nonverbal elements in speech, such as intonation, that may affect the meaning of an utterance 副语言；使用语调等影响话语意思
passivity	n.	the state of accepting what happens without reacting or trying to fight against it 被动；消极状态
pitch	n.	how high or low a sound is, especially a musical note（尤指乐音的）音高
posture	n.	the position in which you hold your body when standing or sitting（站、坐立的）姿势
proxemics	n.	the branch of knowledge that deals with the amount of space that people feel it necessary to set between themselves and others 人际距离学

139

pushy	*adj.*	trying hard to get what you want, especially in a way that seems rude 执意强求的，咄咄逼人的
sarcasm	*n.*	a sharp, bitter, or cutting expression or remark to mock or to convey contempt 讽刺，嘲讽
slouch	*v.*	to stand, sit or move in a lazy way, often with your shoulders and head bent forward 无精打采地站（或坐、走），低头垂肩地站（或坐、走）
squat	*v.*	to sit on your heels with your knees bent up close to your body 蹲坐，蹲
tempo	*n.*	the speed of any movement or activity（运动或活动的）速度；节奏
thrust	*v.*	to push sb./sth. suddenly or violently in a particular direction; to move quickly and suddenly in a particular direction 猛推；冲；戳；挤；塞；(手指) 向上指
uncivilized	*adj.*	not behaving in a way that is acceptable according to social or moral standards 不合社会或道德规范的，无教养的，不文明的
utter	*v.*	to make a sound with your voice; to say sth. 出声，说，讲

Reading Comprehension

I. Choose the best options to answer the following questions or fill in the blank.

1. What is the focus of the text?
   A. Functions of nonverbal communication.
   B. The relationship between verbal communication and nonverbal communication.
   C. The impact of culture on nonverbal communication.
   D. The importance of body language.

2. Which of the following is the function of "nonverbal communication"?
   A. Showing our attitudes.
   B. Marking our identities.

Unit 8 Nonverbal Communication and Culture

   C. Releasing our emotional tension.

   D. All of the above.

3. Which of the following statements is **NOT** true according to the text?

   A. Nonverbal behavior works together with verbal communication.

   B. Nonverbal behavior is independent of verbal communication.

   C. Nonverbal behavior can clarify what the verbal behavior conveys.

   D. Nonverbal behavior and verbal one may contradict each other.

4. Which of the following is **NOT** part of "nonverbal communication"?

   A. Paralanguage.　　　　　　　　B. Written communication.

   C. Kinesics.　　　　　　　　　　D. Proxemics.

5. According to the text, which of the following is true about "V" sign?

   A. "V" sign is a signal for victory in the United States.

   B. "V" sign done with your palm facing yourself is considered rude in England.

   C. "V" sign signals the number "two" in China.

   D. All of the above.

6. Which of the following statements is true according to the text?

   A. In Muslim countries, women and men are encouraged to have eye contact.

   B. To Japanese, silence is a rich communication style and they regard it as a virtue.

   C. North Americans consider direct eye contact as an invasion of one's privacy.

   D. Italian women feel offended when they are gazed at by men.

7. To know another culture well, we should do as the following **EXCEPT** _____.

   A. learning the hidden dimension of communication of that culture

   B. listening to the silent language and read the invisible messages of that culture

   C. understanding the nonverbal behavior of that culture

   D. placing verbal behavior of that culture before its nonverbal behavior

II. Decide whether the following statements are TRUE, FALSE, or NOT GIVEN according to the information given in the text.

1. Speaking is just one mode of communication. There are many others.

2. Most of the time, we use nonverbal communication without being aware of it.
   _____

3. According to some researchers, more information is communicated through verbal means than through nonverbal means.
   _____

4. Body language is the most important part of nonverbal communication.
   _____

5. Laughing or smiling is often used by Japanese men to hide their feelings.
   _____

6. In some cultures, direct eye contact should be avoided in order to show respect or obedience.
   _____

7. American people tend to view silence in communication as necessary and desirable.
   _____

Checking Basic Concepts

Complete the following statements with a proper word or phrase in the box. Each word or phrase can be used only once.

| chronemics | paralanguage | gesture | posture |
| kinesics | proxemics | nonverbal communication | |

1. Communication without the use of words is referred to as _____.

2. Time language, the study of how we use time in communication, is also called _____.

3. _____, including the study of body distance and body touch, is also known as spatial language.

4. The study of body movements and activities in human communication is _____.

Unit 8 Nonverbal Communication and Culture

5. _____ is the way people hold their bodies when they sit, stand or walk.

6. _____ refers to the use of movement of the hands, arms, or head, etc. to express an idea or feeling or attitude.

7. The study of using vocal effects (such as intonation, pitch, volume, tempo) rather than words to convey meaning is known as _____.

Language in Use

I. **Complete the following sentences with the words in the box. Change the form if necessary. Each word can be used only once.**

| count | uncivilized | utter | sarcasm |
| contradict | dictate | integrity | intricacy |

1. The price of this artwork largely depends on the _____ of the work.

2. When we take our vacations is very much _____ by our manager's work schedule.

3. I have always regarded him as a man of _____.

4. The two stories _____ each other.

5. Every point in this game _____, so the players should go all out and struggle for it.

6. I think any sport involving harm to animals is barbaric (野蛮的) and _____.

7. She did not _____ a word during lunch.

8. His book commingles (混合) _____ and sadness.

II. **Paraphrase the following sentences from Text A.**

1. Nonverbal communication is important to the study of intercultural communication because a lack of knowledge of another culture's nonverbal communication patterns may cause serious cultural conflicts.

_____

_____

143

2. Nonverbal behavior also works together with verbal communication. Nonverbal behavior can clarify what the verbal behavior conveys, or they can contradict each other—as happens in sarcasm.

Expanding Intercultural Knowledge

Body Language in Different Cultures

1. The Korean Bow

Western countries reserve the bow for the end of a great stage performance, while bowing is very important in many East Asian cultures, including Japan, China and Korea, among others. In these countries, bowing is part of basic etiquette (礼仪) to show respect and gratitude. In Korea, you bow when initially meeting a person, to say "Hello", to bid "Goodbye", to say "Thank you" and "I'm sorry". Generally, the lower you bow, the more respect and deference (顺从) you show the other person. And the longer you keep your head bowed, the more serious you are.

2. The German "one"

You probably use your fingers to count things, like signaling how many mugs of beer you want. In Germany, if you're not careful, you might get drunk a little bit quicker. Not just because they have huge beer mugs, but because they have a different way of finger counting. In the U.S.A., the number "one" is signified by the pointer finger (食指). In Germany—and a few other European countries like France and Italy—they start counting with the thumb. And the pointer finger signifies "two". If you show the waiter a pointer finger, he might think that you're saying "two" and bring you a pair of those huge mugs.

3. The Indian Head Shake

In Western cultures, when we say "Yes", we nod our heads up and down.

When we say "No", we swing the head from left to right. These gestures aren't universal. In India, "Yes" is expressed by tilting (倾斜) the head from side to side—that is, towards the shoulders. And the faster the shake, the more certain the "Yes" is. This head shake gesture can also be used during a conversation to indicate that the listener is paying attention and being agreeable. Likewise, it can be a sign of courtesy (礼仪) and respect.

4. The Italian Pinecone

As Italians talk practically with their hands, there are probably hundreds of recognizable Italian hand gestures. The most typical of them is the "pinecone" (松果手). With palms up, the pinecone is formed by bringing the tips of all your fingers to a single point. Rock your wrist back and forth, and you have the most recognizable hand gesture in the Italian world. Think of it as the accompanying gesture for asking questions—especially when you're utterly (完全) confused or desperate for the answer, for example: "What were you thinking?" or "What's happening?"

5. The French "So-So"

As connoisseurs (内行) of the good life, the French have high standards for almost everything (not just with food and fashion), so you might hear them often say "Comme ci comme ça", which is the equivalent (同义语) of the English "So-So". When you ask them, for example, how their day went or how the event was, they can tell you it was okay—nothing really memorable or worthy of discussion. This "So-So" answer would often be coupled with a gesture of a palm-down hand rocking from side to side—like a boat rocking back and forth.

6. The Chinese Nose Point

As the most prominent and central part of the face, the nose represents the self in Chinese and other East Asian cultures. So when Chinese people refer to themselves, they don't point to their chest like people in many other cultures. Instead, using the forefinger (食指) or the thumb, they point to the nose. But, pointing at the nose of others is considered extremely rude in China!

7. The Swiss Cheek Kisses

Have you ever been in that awkward situation where you go in for a hug but the other person goes in for a cheek kiss? And by the time you notice, you're not sure which cheek to start with. In Switzerland, it's three cheek kisses—starting with your right cheek. Many countries in Europe and Latin America use cheek kisses as a way of greeting. The Swiss kiss, in particular, is a common way to greet family and close friends—especially when it's between girl-and-girl or girl-and-boy. Between men, not so much—they usually do with a warm handshake, unless they're really close. New acquaintances are welcomed with a handshake but as the relationship deepens, this graduates (升级) to cheek kisses.

8. The Iranian "Thumbs-Up"

In a Western country, if someone on the street gives you a thumbs-up, he/she is probably being friendly and encouraging. That thumbs-up gesture says "Hello, friend! I am in approval of your outfit (服装) or action!" But in many Middle Eastern cultures like Iran, Iraq and parts of Greece, the "thumbs-up" is basically the equivalent of giving someone the middle finger. However, thanks to Hollywood movies, Facebook and other elements of popular culture disseminating (传播) in the Middle East, the thumbs-up gesture can sometimes just be a genuine (真正的) thumbs-up. In fact, several members of Middle Eastern leadership use the gesture themselves to mean "OK" or "cool". So how do you know if the gesture is meant in a positive or negative way? Maybe you never will.

9. The Japanese Eye Contact

Eye contact is a very important component of body language, and different countries give different subtexts (潜台词) to the same action. In many countries, maintaining eye contact while you speak to someone signifies that you're paying attention. (Think of a mother demanding "Look at me when I'm talking to you!") In Japan and a few other East Asian cultures, however, eye contact can signal aggression and disrespect. In fact, many Japanese people are taught at an early age to look at the necks of people instead of looking into their eyes. However, nowadays it's becoming more socially acceptable to look people in the eyes when you're talking to them.

10. The Russian Finger Count

Here we have another method of counting that probably differs from the way you're familiar with. Count with your fingers from one to five. Chances are, you started with a balled-up (卷成一团的) fist and gradually uncurled (展开) each finger as you went along the numbers. You'll be glad to know that in Russia, people also count with their fingers. But instead of starting with a closed fist, they start with an open palm. To count to five, for example, Russians open their palm then, sometimes with the help of the pointer finger on their other hand, curl in their pinky finger (小拇指), followed by the ring finger (无名指) and so on. By "five", they'd have a balled-up fist.

By now, you should understand how important and how different body language is for different cultures. Learning the specific gestures and movements for the particular language you are studying is a big help in communicating with clarity and effectiveness.

(Source: Stevie Tan, *Body Language in Different Cultures*)

Reflecting and Discussing

1. Which of the above-mentioned body languages impresses you most?
2. Compare and contrast Chinese and Russian ways of counting fingers.

Understanding Personal Space Across Cultures

Read **Text B** and do the exercises online.

Case Study

Discuss with your classmates the questions according to each case.

 Case 1

Noir's TV commercial

Drakkar Noir, the men's aftershave fragrance, was launched by Guy LaRoche in 1982 in France. In order to appeal to adventurous, passionate and modern male customers, the company designed a TV commercial in which a woman clutched (抓住) the bare arm of a man who was holding a bottle of Drakkar Noir in his hand. Since this commercial almost guaranteed a scent (香味) that would be rich, sophisticated, and irresistible to the ladies, the promotion of Drakkar Noir turned out to be very successful.

Later on, the company decided to use the same commercial to open its Middle Eastern market. Unfortunately, the promotion soon became a disaster. After a flurry (一阵) of market research, the company realized the impropriety of the body language used in the commercial to a Saudi Arabian audience, and soon replaced it with a woman using the tip of her finger to slightly touch a man's arm in a suit. With this change in body language, the campaign finally led to a good year for sales in this new market.

(Source: Dou Weilin, *Introduction to Intercultural Communication*)

1. Why did the Drakkar Noir company design the TV commercial in which a woman clutched the bare arm of a man?

2. Why was the body language used in the first commercial inappropriate to a Saudi Arabian audience?

3. What change did the company make to the commercial? What was the consequence of the change?

 Case 2

Agree or Disagree?

Two co-workers, Li Yang (Chinese) and Tom Smith (from New Zealand)

Unit 8 Nonverbal Communication and Culture

are discussing an engineering project. As Tom puts forward his ideas, Li keeps nodding his head and saying, "Um" "Yes" and "Uh huh". When Tom finishes and asks about Li's comment, he merely replies: "I really don't think that project will work." Feeling upset, Tom asks, "Then why did you pretend to agree the whole time?" Li feels completely confused and asks, "What makes you think that I was agreeing with you?"

(Source: Huang Yucai, *A New Comparison of English and Chinese Languages and Cultures*)

What do you think caused the misunderstanding?

Unit 9 Intercultural Conflict Management

Don't be afraid of opposition. Remember, a kite rises against, not with, the wind.
—Hamilton W. Mabie

礼之用,和为贵。
——《论语》

Learning Objectives

Upon completion of this unit, you will be able to:

- Identify the two orientations to *conflict*.
- Explain the five conflict management styles.
- Discuss the impact of value differences on conflict styles.
- Assess your own specific conflict styles.
- Understand how and why conflict occurs, and the impact of conflict on work and interpersonal relationships.
- Know how to make conflict productive and avoid unnecessary conflict.
- Understand, interpret and critically evaluate different cultural behaviors.

 **Lead-in**

What Would You Do?

Situation 1

You're walking along on a train when you knock over someone's coffee. What would you say?

    A. Say nothing, and walk away.

    B. "It's not my fault! That was a stupid place to put it."

    C. "I'm terribly sorry."

    D. "Sorry. Are you OK? I'll get you another one."

Situation 2

Your company has a no-smoking policy, which you agree with. A visitor walks into your office and lights a cigarette. What would you say?

    A. "Smoking causes cancer."

    B. "You're not allowed to smoke here."

Unit 9 Intercultural Conflict Management

C. "I hope you don't mind, but I'm afraid we have a no-smoking policy here."

D. Say nothing, and let him smoke.

Situation 3

You're in a hotel and the TV in the neighboring room is very loud. You're trying to get to sleep. What would you do?

A. Knock on the wall with your shoe, and shout "Turn down the TV! I'm trying to sleep!"

B. Call the reception desk and ask the hotel staff to request your neighbor to turn their TV down.

C. Knock on the door of the neighboring room and say, "I'm sorry, but your TV's rather loud and I'm trying to sleep. Would you mind turning it down?"

D. Do nothing, and try to get to sleep.

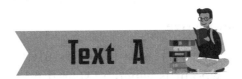

Culture, Communication and Conflict

1   The need to understand intercultural conflict seems more important now than ever. One thing we can be sure of is that conflict is inevitable. *Conflicts* are happening all around the world, as they always have, and at many different levels: interpersonal, social, national, and international. Understanding intercultural conflict is especially important because of the relationship between culture and conflict. That is, cultural differences can cause conflict, and once conflict occurs, cultural backgrounds and experiences influence how individuals deal with it.

Two Orientations to Conflict

2   Is conflict good or bad? Should conflict be welcomed because it provides opportunities to strengthen relationships? Or should it be avoided because it can only lead to problems for individuals and groups? What is the best way to handle conflict when it arises? Should people talk about it directly, deal with it indirectly, or avoid it?

3 It's not always easy to figure out the best way to deal with conflict. And what does culture have to do with it? To answer some of these questions, we first describe two very different ways of thinking about conflict. As you read about these two orientations, try to keep in mind the importance of thinking **dialectically**. Neither orientation is always the best **approach**, nor does any culture only utilize one approach to conflict.

A. Conflict as Opportunity

4 The "opportunity" orientation to conflict is the one most commonly represented in U.S. interpersonal communication. Conflict is usually defined as involving a perceived or real **incompatibility** of goals, values, expectations, processes, or outcomes between two or more interdependent individuals or groups. This approach to conflict is based on four **assumptions**: firstly, conflict is a normal, useful process; secondly, all issues are subject to change through negotiation; thirdly, direct confrontation and **conciliation** are valued; and finally, conflict is a **redistribution** of opportunity, release of tensions, and **renewal** of relationships. This Western-based approach to conflict suggests a **neutral**-to-positive orientation, but it is not shared by all cultural groups.

B. Conflict as Destructive

5 Many cultural groups view conflict as ultimately unproductive for relationships. This viewpoint is generally shared by many Asian cultures. Four assumptions underlie this perspective. First, conflict is a destructive disturbance of the peace; second, the social system should not be adjusted to meet the needs of members; rather, members should adapt to established values; third, confrontations are destructive and ineffective; last, **disputants** should be **disciplined**.

Conflict Management Styles

6 Depending on how individuals balance the incompatibility of goals and feel the desire to serve the needs and goals of their own versus those of other parties involved in the conflict, there are at least five specific styles of managing conflicts, as illustrated in the figure on the next page.

Unit 9 Intercultural Conflict Management

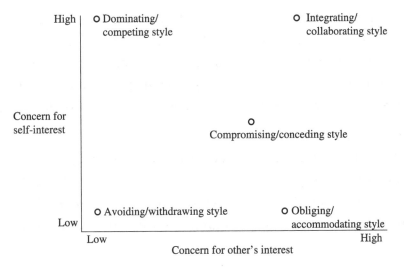

(Source: Ting-Toomey & Chung, 2012)

7   The *avoiding/withdrawing* *style* is adopted when individuals prefer simply not to confront the other party, such as someone who has offended them, perhaps because of fear of the consequences resulting from a direct confrontation of the issue. Avoiding issues may work in the short term, but it is not productive for long-term relationships. This style may be useful, however, when less **is at stake**, when the issue is **trivial**, when the issue can be managed with other (indirect) approaches, when you have no chance of winning, or sometimes just to let the offending party cool down.

8   The *obliging/accommodating style* describes a situation in which one person **gives in** to the demands of the other party. This often requires the sacrifice of personal goals for the resolution of conflict and the maintenance of a harmonious relationship. Such sacrifices take the form of **appeasement**, abandoning one's principles for the greater good of the relationship in that context, and not minding one's own personal discomfort at the **going-along-to-get-along** mindset. This style can be used successfully when you find yourself in the wrong, when the issue of conflict is not as personally significant to you as it may be to the other party, and when harmony, peaceful coexistence and collaboration are more important than individual success.

9   The *dominating/competing style* describes a win-lose situation, working on the assumption that for one party to succeed, the other necessarily has to lose or fail. It is a style characterized by aggressive behavior, overt disagreement, and extreme **assertiveness**, to the discomfort of the other party. A competing style can seriously damage relationships, put the parties into an attack–counterattack

mode, and leave them angered, disrespected, and **humiliated**, with no intentions of seeking a cooperative solution. But if time **is of the essence** and a quick decision needs to be made, or when unpopular actions need to be **implemented**, or there is a threat of competitors taking advantage of your accommodating or collaborating efforts, this style may be the best and only option to exercise.

10   The *integrating/collaborating style* describes a win-win situation, working best when parties **are committed to** collaborating and resolving conflicts. This style encourages **disgruntled** parties to engage in dialog and work together to develop mutually beneficial solutions. However, arriving at a **consensual** and mutually acceptable solution is often challenging, emotionally **exhausting**, and time-consuming.

11   The *compromising/conceding style* is considered, a middle-ground approach, being more assertive than avoiding or accommodating but less confrontational than competing. In this approach, parties seek a solution collaboratively, usually with both parties gaining some objectives but not all of them. Although each party gains something in this approach, some see it as a lose-lose situation, because in order for conflicting parties to **compromise** and reach an agreement, they both have to give up something. A compromise is often **triggered** by self-interest, since parties act in ways that are most beneficial to themselves. This style may be used most effectively when parties are committed to mutually exclusive goals and when the **temporary** resolution of the dispute is more important than a long-term **permanent** solution.

Value Differences and Conflict Styles

12   Looking at how cultural values influence conflict management styles is a good way to understand cultural variations. Cultural values in individualistic societies differ from those in collectivistic societies. Individualistic societies place greater importance on the individual than on groups like the family or the work group. In contrast, collectivistic societies often place greater importance on extended families and loyalty to groups.

13   These contrasting values may influence communication patterns. People from individualistic societies tend to be more concerned with saving their own face and **dignity** than others', so they tend to use more controlling, confrontational, and solution-oriented conflict management styles. In contrast, people from collectivistic societies tend to be more concerned with preserving

Unit 9　Intercultural Conflict Management

group harmony and with saving the face of the other party during conflict. They may use a less direct conversational style; protecting the other person's face and making him or her look good is considered a skillful facework style. These face concerns lead them to use more avoiding, accommodating, and integrating conflict styles. However, some evidence indicates that not all collectivistic societies prefer indirect ways of dealing with conflict. How someone chooses to deal with conflict in any situation depends on the type of conflict and the relationship he/she has with the other party.

14　One study found that Japanese college students tended to use the avoiding style more often with **acquaintances** than with best friends in some types of conflicts (conflicts of values and opinions). In contrast, they used the integrating style more with best friends than with acquaintances. In interest conflicts, they used a dominating style more with acquaintances than with best friends. This suggests that with outgroup members, as with acquaintances, for whom harmony is not as important, the Japanese tend to use dominating or avoiding styles (depending on the conflict type). However, with ingroup members like best friends, the way to maintain harmony is to work through the conflict with an integrating style.

(Source: Judith N. Martin & Thomas K. Nakayama, *Intercultural Communication in Contexts*, Chapter 8 and John R. Baldwin et al., *Intercultural Communication for Everyday Life*, Chapter 12)

New Words

accommodating	*adj.*	helpful and willing to do what someone else wants 随和的
acquaintance	*n.*	a person that you know but who is not a close friend 认识的人，泛泛之交；熟人
appeasement	*n.*	giving people what they want to prevent them from harming you or being angry with you 姑息；安抚
approach	*n.*	a way of dealing with sb./sth.; a way of doing or thinking about sth. such as a problem or a task（待人接物或思考问题的）方式，方法，态度

assertiveness	n.	the quality of being confident and not frightened to say what you want or believe 自信；坚定
assumption	n.	a belief or feeling that sth. is true or that sth. will happen, although there is no proof 假定，假设
compromise	v.	to give up some of your demands after a disagreement with sb. in order to reach an agreement（为达成协议而）妥协，折中，让步
concede	v.	to give sth. away, especially unwillingly; to allow sb. to have sth.（尤指勉强地）让与，让步；允许
conciliation	n.	willingness to end a disagreement or the process of ending a disagreement 和解意愿；和解
consensual	adj.	based on general agreement among all the members of a group 一致同意的
dialectically	adv.	in a manner related to or characteristic of dialectics, which is a method of argument for resolving disagreements and exploring the truth of complex issues through logical discussion and reasoning 辩证的
dignity	n.	a calm and serious manner that deserves respect 庄重，庄严，尊严
discipline	v.	to punish sb. for sth. he/she has done 惩罚，处罚
disgruntled	adj.	annoyed or disappointed because sth. has happened to upset you 不满的，不高兴的
disputant	n.	one that is engaged in dispute 争论者，争执者
exhausting	adj.	making you feel very tired 使人疲惫不堪的，令人筋疲力尽的
humiliate	v.	to make sb. feel ashamed or stupid and lose the respect of other people 羞辱，使丧失尊严
implement	v.	to make sth. that has been officially decided start to happen or be used 使生效；贯彻，执行，实施
incompatibility	n.	the quality of being unable to exist or work in congenial combination 不相容

Unit 9 Intercultural Conflict Management

neutral	*adj.*	not supporting or helping either side in a disagreement, competition, etc. 中立的，持平的，无倾向性的
obliging	*adj.*	willing and eager to help 乐于助人的
permanent	*adj.*	lasting for a long time or for all time in the future; existing all the time 永久的，永恒的，长久的
redistribution	*n.*	the act of redistributing sth., especially money or land 重新分配
renewal	*n.*	a situation in which sth. begins again after a pause or an interruption 恢复，重新开始；更新
temporary	*adj.*	lasting or intended to last or be used only for a short time; not permanent 短暂的，暂时的，临时的
trigger	*v.*	to make sth. happen suddenly 发动，引起，触发
trivial	*adj.*	not important or serious; not worth considering 不重要的，琐碎的，微不足道的
withdraw	*v.*	to become quieter and spend less time with other people 不与人交往

Useful Expressions

be at stake	to be at risk 处于险境
be committed to	to promise sincerely that you will definitely do sth., keep to an agreement or arrangement, etc. 承诺，保证（做某事、遵守协议或遵从安排等）
be of the essence	to be absolutely necessary in order for a particular action to be successful 极重要的，关键的
give in	to cease fighting or arguing; to admit defeat 屈服，让步
going-along-to-get-along	agreeing with others or doing what they want to preserve harmony 得过且过；委曲求全

Reading Comprehension

I. Choose the best options to answer the following questions or fill in the blanks.

1. According to Paragraph 1, conflicts can be _____.
   A. inevitable and universal
   B. national and international
   C. interpersonal and social
   D. all of the above

2. Which of the following statements is true about the two orientations to conflict?
   A. Western cultures tend to view conflict as destructive for relationships.
   B. People from Asian countries value conflict and are more likely to view it as an opportunity.
   C. One could not rely on one single approach to handling conflicts when they arise.
   D. There's no chance that the issues rising from conflicts can be changed through negotiation.

3. Which of the following strategies for dealing with conflicts is the most aggressive?
   A. Avoiding.
   B. Accommodating.
   C. Competing.
   D. Compromising.

4. Suppose you are arguing with your roommate over the constant noises he made with his music band at late night, but he leaves before you finish the talk. The roommate's departure illustrates the _____ conflict resolution style.
   A. avoiding
   B. accommodating
   C. competing
   D. collaborating

5. Which of the following statements might be true about the conflict management style utilized in the scenario described in Question 4?
   A. "You" try to reach a compromise with the roommate.
   B. The roommate leaves so as not to create any unnecessary confrontation.
   C. The roommate is sacrificing his own interests for the resolution of conflicts.
   D. The roommate is abandoning his own principles for the good of their relationship.

Unit 9　Intercultural Conflict Management

6. Which of the following statements about the five conflict styles is true?
   A. The competing style is efficient only when a quick decision needs to be made.
   B. When conflicting parties engage themselves in dialog and work together, they are more likely to arrive at mutually beneficial solutions.
   C. Avoiding approach can resolve conflicts in the long run.
   D. The conflicting parties can hardly gain any objectives if they compromise.

7. _____ is more likely to create a win-win situation.
   A. Avoiding   B. Accommodating
   C. Competing   D. Collaborating

II. **Decide whether the following statements are TRUE, FALSE, or NOT GIVEN according to the information given in the text.**

1. People from different cultural backgrounds may view conflicts differently.

2. Conflicts as destructive orientation are common in U.S. interpersonal communication contexts.

3. A competing style is often characterized by aggressive behavior and is always damaging.

4. The disadvantages of the competing or dominating style outweigh its advantages in dealing with conflicts.

5. Individualistic societies attach greater importance to individuals than families or work groups.

6. People from collectivistic societies tend to use more avoiding, accommodating and integrating conflict styles to deal with conflicts.

7. Japanese college students prefer a competing or dominating style with friends in interest conflicts.

Checking Basic Concepts

Complete the following statements with a proper word in the box. Each word can be used only once.

| accommodating | avoiding | conflict |
| collaborating | compromising | competing |

1. A(n) _____ is a situation in which people, groups or countries are involved in a serious disagreement or argument.

2. _____ is a style characterized by aggressive behavior, overt disagreement, and extreme assertiveness, to the discomfort of the other party.

3. The _____ style encourages both parties to engage in dialog and work together to develop mutually beneficial solutions.

4. The _____ style involves sharing and exchanging information in such a way that both individuals give up something to find a mutually acceptable solution.

5. The face concerns lead people from collectivistic societies to use more _____, accommodating, and integrating conflict styles.

6. The _____ style often requires the sacrifice of personal goals for the resolution of conflict and maintaining of a harmonious relationship.

Language in Use

I. **Complete the following sentences with the words in the box. Change the form if necessary. Each word can be used only once.**

| approach | withdraw | trivial | permanent |
| discipline | neutral | compromise | trigger |

1. Research shows that many depressed people tend to _____ into themselves.

2. It is a(n) _____ matter and not worth fighting about.

3. A series of _____ should be adopted to protect the cultural heritages from extinction.

Unit 9 Intercultural Conflict Management

4. Switzerland was _____ during the war.

5. According to school rules and regulations, students' misbehavior should be harshly _____.

6. Encourage your child to reach a(n) _____ between what he wants and what you want.

7. They had entered the country and had applied for _____ residence.

8. It is still not clear what events _____ off the demonstrations (示威).

II. Paraphrase the following sentences from Text A.

1. Conflicts are happening all around the world, as they always have, and at many different levels: interpersonal, social, national, and international.

   _____
   _____
   _____

2. Individualistic societies place greater importance on the individual than on groups like the family or the work group. In contrast, collectivistic societies often place greater importance on extended families and loyalty to groups.

   _____
   _____
   _____

Expanding Intercultural Knowledge

Assessing Your Specific Five Conflict Styles

Instructions: Recall how you generally communicate in various conflict situations with acquaintances. Let your first response be your guide and circle the number in the scale that best reflects your conflict style tendency. The following scale is used for each item:

4 = SA = strongly agree—IT'S ME!

3 = MA = moderately agree—It's kind of like me.

2 = MD = moderately disagree—It's kind of not me.

1 = SD = strongly disagree—IT'S NOT ME!

	SA	MA	MD	SD
1. I often "grin and bear it" when the other person does something I don't like.	4	3	2	1
2. I "give and take" so that a compromise can be reached.	4	3	2	1
3. I use my influence to get my ideas accepted in resolving the problem.	4	3	2	1
4. I am open to the other person's suggestions in resolving the problem.	4	3	2	1
5. I generally give in to the wishes of the other person in a conflict.	4	3	2	1
6. I usually avoid open discussion of the conflict with the person.	4	3	2	1
7. I try to find a middle course to break an impasse (僵局).	4	3	2	1
8. I argue the case with the other person to show the merits of my position.	4	3	2	1
9. I integrate my viewpoints with the other person to achieve a joint resolution.	4	3	2	1
10. I generally try to satisfy the expectations of the other person.	4	3	2	1
11. I try not to bump up against the other person whenever possible.	4	3	2	1
12. I try to play down our differences to reach a compromise.	4	3	2	1
13. I'm generally firm in pursuing my side of the issue.	4	3	2	1
14. I encourage the other person to try to see things from a creative angle.	4	3	2	1

Unit 9 Intercultural Conflict Management

15. I often go along with the suggestions of the other person.	4	3	2	1
16. I usually bear my resentment in silence.	4	3	2	1
17. I usually propose a middle ground for breaking deadlocks (僵局).	4	3	2	1
18. I am emotionally expressive in the conflict situation.	4	3	2	1
19. I communicate with the other person with close attention to her or his needs.	4	3	2	1
20. I do my best to accommodate the wishes of the other person in a conflict.	4	3	2	1

Scoring:

Add up the scores on items 1, 6, 11, and 16 and you will find your **avoiding** conflict style score. Avoiding style score: _____.

Add up the scores on items 2, 7, 12, and 17 and you will find your **compromising** conflict style score. Compromising style score: _____.

Add up the scores on items 3, 8, 13, and 18 and you will find your **dominating** conflict style score. Dominating style score: _____.

Add up the scores on items 4, 9, 14, and 19 and you will find your **integrating** conflict style score. Integrating style score: _____.

Add up the scores on items 5, 10, 15, and 20 and you will find your **accommodating** conflict style score. Accommodating style score: _____.

Interpretation: Scores on each conflict style dimension can range from 4 to 16; the higher the score, the more you engage in that particular conflict style. If some of the scores are similar on some of the conflict style dimensions, you tend to use a mixed pattern of different conflict styles.

(Source: Stella Ting-Toomey & Leeva C. Chung,
Understanding Intercultural Communication)

Reflecting and Discussing

Compare your conflict style scores with those of a classmate. Take a moment to think about the following questions, and discuss them with your classmates.

1. Where did you learn your conflict style tendencies?
2. What do you think are the pros and cons of each specific conflict style?
3. When you are having a conflict with someone from a different culture, how would you address the different conflict style issues? What skills do you need to practice more to be a culturally sensitive conflict negotiator?

How and Why Does Conflict Occur?

Read Text B and do the exercises online.

Unit 9 Intercultural Conflict Management

 Case Study

Discuss with your classmates the questions according to each case.

 Case 1

Your Project or Our Project?

Yoko, a Japanese student, recounted a conflict she had with an American student, Linda, with whom she was working on a class project. Linda seemed to take a very competitive, individualistic approach to the project, saying things like "I did this on the project" or referring to it as "my project". Yoko became increasingly irritated and less motivated to work on the project. She finally said to Linda, "Is this your project or our project?" Linda seemed surprised and didn't apologize; she only defended herself. The two women continued to work on the project but with a strained (紧张的) relationship.

(Source: Judith N. Martin & Thomas K. Nakayama, *Intercultural Communication in Contexts*)

1. Who do you think is responsible for their strained relationship and why?

2. If you were one of the students, how would you approach the conflict and manage to resolve it?

 Case 2

Chinese Grandpa in America

For most elderly Chinese living in the United States, one of their main responsibilities is to help take care of their grandchildren. Since most of their grandchildren were born and grew up in America, it's not an easy job for them.

When Mr. Xin arrived in America, he was very happy to meet Mike, his ten-year-old grandson, who had been born in America. His son, who was educated according to the traditional "beating" principle of China, warned Mr. Xin that according to the local law, physical punishment of children was forbidden. Mr. Xin always remembered this caution until one day, during lunchtime, Mr. Xin couldn't control himself when Mike, who hated vegetables, picked out all the vegetables from his plate and threw them aside. Spanked by his grandfather for the first time, Mike didn't cry. He went to pick up the telephone and called the police. Mr. Xin thought Mike was calling his mother, and was shocked when a police car arrived at the door fifteen minutes later.

(Source: Fan Weiwei, *A Multimedia Approach to Intercultural Communication*)

1. What contributed to the conflict between Mr. Xin and his American grandson?

2. If you were the son of Mr. Xin, how would you resolve the problem?

Unit 10 Intercultural Adaptation

The world is a book and those who do not travel read only one page.
—Saint Augustine

橘生淮南则为橘,生于淮北则为枳。

——《晏子春秋》

Learning Objectives

Upon completion of this unit, you will be able to:

- Understand the nature of *culture shock* and *intercultural adaptation*.
- Describe the symptoms and effects of *culture shock*.
- Distinguish between the U-curve and W-curve patterns of *intercultural adaptation*.
- Evaluate your adaptative potential.
- Understand the vulnerability of international students and the importance to accept and learn from it.
- Analyze communicative failures critically.
- Use a range of strategies to cope with adaptation stress.

 **Lead-in**

Doubts

Wu Lian, an English major studying at a university in the U.S., starts out confidently. She knows that her language skills are better than those of many Chinese studying abroad. At first, everything is fine, but gradually she discovers that professors do not always present material in an organized way, nor do they always speak clearly. Some are from other countries and speak English with a foreign accent; others talk so fast that she cannot keep up. They expect her to read a whole book every week for each class! Several of her courses require her to write term papers longer than her graduation thesis (论文). The library is so big and complex and lists so many resources on the assigned topics that she wonders how she will manage to do the necessary research.

Wu Lian finds she cannot understand the group conversations of her native-speaking classmates. They use a lot of slang (俚语), make jokes she does not understand, and convey much of their meaning with subtle gestures she cannot decode. Some treat her kindly but like an incapable child; others expect her to know everything and feel and do as they do. The way they talk about "partying" frightens her. They sometimes invite her to join in their social activities, but she has neither the time nor the money to participate.

In the meantime, she gets letters from her family and friends at home, expressing their pride and confidence in her. Her parents tell her to work hard and take care of her health. She studies more hours a day than anyone she knows. Fresh fruits and vegetables are so expensive, and the food in the dining hall is so unappetizing. Why don't they have street sellers here? She would like to cut costs by cooking for herself, but the local convenience store does not sell vegetables and it takes too long to get to the supermarket by bus.

Wu Lian writes to her parents, but what she tells them is not what she really feels.

(Source: Linell Davis, *Doing Culture: Cross-Cultural Communication in Action*)

Questions for Intercultural Understanding

1. What problems and difficulties does Wu Lian encounter when studying in the U.S.?

2. If you were her, would you meet any other difficulties and challenges?

3. What suggestions would you give to help her cope with those difficulties?

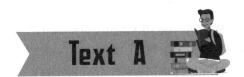

Adapting to a New Culture

1   Perhaps you have traveled to another country or region during school holidays or as an exchange student. Maybe you have visited a different culture within your own country. In such cases, you may have experienced difficulty. However, the difficulties we feel during short-term trips differ from those felt by *sojourners*—those who travel abroad for a longer time, say one to five years, with the intent to return home, such as diplomats, international students, military **personnel** on foreign duty, business persons on assignment abroad—or new immigrants, or **refugees**.

2   When individuals move from their home cultures to a new culture, they take with them their cultural habits, and interaction routines. For the most part, these old cultural habits may produce unintended clashes in the new culture. This can result in **disorientation**, misunderstandings, conflict, stress, and anxiety.

Researchers call this phenomenon *culture shock*.

Culture Shock and Intercultural Adaptation

3   *Intercultural adaptation* refers broadly to the process of increasing our level of fitness to meet the demands of a new cultural environment. It deals with how sojourners or new immigrants experience the **distress** caused by **mismatches** or incompatibility between the *host culture*—the new culture they move to—and the culture of birth. In other words, intercultural adaptation is a process of dealing with **maladjustment** within a host culture. Entrance into a new culture is generally accompanied by culture shock. We are unlikely to experience it suddenly, from a single event. More likely we will feel it gradually, from our experience of navigating a different cultural environment **day in and day out**.

Symptoms of Culture Shock

4   The reactions to culture shock may differ greatly from person to person. For some, it may take only a few weeks to work through the psychological distress due to the cultural differences they experience; for others, however, it may take a long period of time to overcome the frustration of culture shock. In very serious cases, the only way to eliminate the problem caused by culture shock may be to return to familiar surroundings.

5   It is reported that **symptoms** of culture shock include depression, helplessness, **hostility** to the host country, feelings of anxiety, homesickness, loneliness, **paranoid** feelings, lack of confidence, **irritability**, confusion, disorientation, isolation, intolerance of **ambiguity** and impatience.

Effects of Culture Shock

6   Culture shock can be viewed as a transitional process in which sojourners gradually become aware of and begin to adjust to cultural differences in a new environment. This process may lead to either of the two directions, depending on individual personality.

7   In a positive sense, culture shock may contribute to individual growth. First, culture shock provides a learning opportunity that demands new responses from sojourners in coping with a constantly changing environment. Second, because most people have a tendency to pursue unique and special goals, culture shock can create an environment and serve as a motivational force for us to move to a new level of **self-actualization**.

8   Third, culture shock can give sojourners a welcome sense of challenge and

Unit 10 Intercultural Adaptation

achievement as a result of dealing with people from very different backgrounds. Fourth, the amount of learning increases when the level of personal anxiety is aroused to a certain degree. To most of us, culture shock offers us a high but not extreme level of anxiety that causes us to learn about a new culture and about ourselves. Finally, the experience from culture shock produces new ideas that, in turn, offer us a new set of behavioral responses for future unfamiliar situations. Our sojourn strengthens us in the future by teaching us how to learn from negative cultural feedback and how to deal with cultures we have not yet experienced.

9   Culture shock may also lead to negative consequences. First, **affectively**, culture shock constitutes an imbalanced experience. On one day, we may experience the mood of **mania** and excitement, while on another, we may feel **hysteria**, confusion, anxiety and depression. This uncertainty may **be detrimental to** the psychological growth of some sojourners. Second, **cognitively** and perceptually, a set of desirable or proper behavior in one culture might be considered bizarre in another. Sorting through feelings about cultural differences may take a long time or may prove impossible for some sojourners.

Stages of Intercultural Adaptation

10   Over the last few decades, scholars have tried to identify stages in the intercultural adaptation process. Among the research on this area, U-curve and W-curve patterns are two popular models used to explain the developmental stages of intercultural adaptation.

   A. U-Curve Pattern

11   Based on a study of 200 Norwegian (挪威的) Fulbright scholars[1], Sverre Lysgaard (1955) developed the well-known U-curve pattern of cultural adjustment. Generally, the U-curve pattern **comprises** four stages: honeymoon period, crisis period, adjustment period, and mastery period.

12   The *honeymoon stage* is the initial period of intercultural adaptation. This stage is a time of happiness and excitement as one first arrives into a new culture. Everything is new and fresh, and even aspects that may not be enjoyable are regarded as great experiences of traveling to a new culture.

13   The second stage, often called the *crisis stage*, represents a time of difficulty as sojourners must directly face the challenges of the new culture on a daily basis. Activities that we **take for granted** suddenly become insurmountable problems.

Such problems often lead to a feeling of rejecting or being rejected by the host culture. Sojourners might spend lots of time alone, become depressed, or spend time only with people from their own culture.

14 Most sojourners work through the difficulties and gradually arrive at the third stage, the *adjustment stage*. Efforts to cope with the problems encountered in the crisis period gradually provide sojourners with new ways to live in the new culture. They begin to learn how to respond and adapt appropriately to the new environment by following the social and cultural norms of the host nation. Sojourners now regain a certain degree of effectiveness, relaxation, and comfort, and have less difficulty **accommodating** both the positive and negative aspects of the host culture.

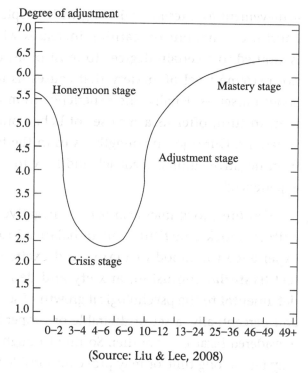

(Source: Liu & Lee, 2008)

15 The *mastery* stage is the last one of the U-curve pattern. In this stage, sojourners may still experience occasional anxiety and frustration, but they have cultivated an understanding of the host culture and can begin to work and play in the new environment with a feeling of enjoyment. They have recovered or nearly recovered from the symptoms of culture shock.

B. W-Curve Pattern

16 If sojourners decide to remain in the host nation, the adaptation process usually ends at the last stage of the U-curve pattern. But if they plan to return to their home countries, they may face a similar process of adaptation to their own cultures. Some scholars extend the U-curve pattern to W-curve to describe the process of *reentry* or *reverse culture shock*. W-curve represents the pattern of readjustment to sojourners' home cultures.

17 The idea of the W-curve is that as sojourners anticipate coming home, they are excited, looking forward to some of the things they missed, and seeing people

Unit 10 Intercultural Adaptation

they love. But after some time, they may feel frustrated, angry or lonely if friends and family don't understand what they experienced or how they have changed. They may miss the host culture and friends, and may look for ways to return. Gradually, they manage to adjust to life at home. Things start to seem normal and routine again, although not exactly the same, and finally they **incorporate** what they have learned and experienced abroad **into** their new life and career.

(Source: Guo-Ming Chen & Willian J. Starosta, *Foundations of Intercultural Communication*, Chapter 8 and John R. Baldwin et al., *Intercultural Communication for Everyday Life*, Chapter 12)

New Words

accommodate	v.	to change your behavior so that you can deal with a new situation better 顺应，适应（新情况）
affectively	adv.	in a manner related to or concerning emotions feelings or the expression of one's emotional state 涉及情感地
ambiguity	n.	the state of being difficult to understand or explain because of involving many different aspects 模棱两可，不明确
cognitively	adv.	in a way that is connected with thinking, or conscious mental processes 认知地，认知上
comprise	v.	to have sb./sth. as parts or members 包括，包含，由……组成
disorientation	n.	a feeling of being confused about where you are, where you are going or what is happening 迷失方向，迷惑
distress	n.	a feeling of great worry or unhappiness; great suffering 忧虑，悲伤，痛苦
hostility	n.	unfriendly or aggressive feelings or behavior 敌意，对抗
hysteria	n.	a state of extreme excitement, fear or anger in which a person, or a group of people, loses control of their emotions and starts to cry, laugh, etc. 歇斯底里，情绪狂暴不可抑止
irritability	n.	the quality of becoming annoyed very easily 易怒
maladjustment	n.	a failure to meet the demands of society, such as coping with problems and social relationships, usually reflected in emotional instability 对社会的不适应

mania	n.	an extremely strong desire or enthusiasm for sth., often shared by a lot of people at the same time（通常指许多人共有的）强烈的欲望，狂热，极大的热情
mismatch	n.	a combination of things or people that do not go together well or are not suitable for each other 误配，错配，搭配不当
paranoid	adj.	afraid or suspicious of other people and believing that they are trying to harm you, in a way that is not reasonable 多疑的，恐惧的
personnel	n.	the people who work for an organization or one of the armed forces（组织或军队中的）全体人员，职员
refugee	n.	a person who has been forced to leave their homes or their country, either because there is a war there, because of their political or religious beliefs, or because of natural disaster 难民
self-actualization	n.	the fact of using your skills and abilities and achieving as much as you can possibly achieve 自我实现（利用自身技能取得尽可能大的成就）
sojourner	n.	a person who has a temporary stay in a place away from home 逗留者；旅居者
symptom	n.	a sign that sth. exists, especially sth. bad 征候，征兆

Useful Expressions

be detrimental to	to be bad for; to be harmful to, to tend to cause harm 对……有害的
day in and day out	everyday, day and night 天天，夜以继日
incorporate into	to include sth. so that it forms a part of sth. 将……包括在内，包含；吸收；使并入
take (sth.) for granted	to accept sth. without question or objection 认为……是理所当然的

Unit 10 Intercultural Adaptation

Cultural Note

1. Fulbright scholars

Each year roughly 850 faculty and professionals from around the world receive Fulbright Scholar (富布莱特访问学者) awards for advanced research and university lecturing in the United States. Individual awards are available to scholars from over 100 countries.

Reading Comprehension

I. **Choose the best options to answer the following questions or fill in the blank.**

1. What is mainly discussed in the text?
   A. How to identify the symptoms of culture shock.
   B. How to understand cultural shock and intercultural adaptation.
   C. How to define culture shock.
   D. How to interpret the U-curve pattern and W-curve pattern.

2. What do sojourners have to experience when they suffer from culture shock?
   A. Disorientation and confusion.   B. Anxiety and stress.
   C. Isolation and loneliness.   D. All of the above.

3. Which of the following about the effects of culture shock is **NOT** mentioned in the text?
   A. Culture shock may contribute to individual growth.
   B. Culture shock can be detrimental to the psychological growth of sojourners.
   C. Culture shock can facilitate one's self-actualization.
   D. Culture shock may damage the physical health of sojourners.

4. What does the phrase in bold in the following sentence probably refer to?
   "***This uncertainty*** *can be detrimental to the psychological growth of the sojourners.*" (Paragraph 9)
   A. One's sojourn might increase the level of his or her personal anxiety.
   B. One's sojourn might expose him or her to more unfamiliar situations.

C. One's imbalanced experience in different cultures makes one feel excited and thrilled one day, yet depressed another.

D. One's desirable, or proper behavior may be considered bizarre in another.

5. What characterize the "adjustment period" in the U-curve pattern?

   A. Sojourners experience heightened anxiety and frustration.

   B. Sojourners regain a sense of effectiveness, relaxation and comfort.

   C. Sojourners feel excitement and novelty about the host culture.

   D. Sojourners undergo psychological distress and rejection.

6. Which of the following statements about the four stages of the U-curve is **NOT** true?

   A. The honeymoon stage is the initial period of culture shock.

   B. Sojourners might experience the fear of being rejected at the crisis stage.

   C. Sojourners have more difficulty coping with problems in the host culture at the adjustment stage.

   D. During the mastery stage, sojourners are expected to recover from the symptoms of culture shock.

7. The W-curve pattern is used by some scholars to describe _____.

   A. reverse culture shock   B. reentry shock
   C. culture shock   D. both A and B

II. Decide whether the following statements are TRUE, FALSE, or NOT GIVEN according to the information given in the text.

1. Sojourners refer to those who travel abroad and live temporarily in one place.

2. Intercultural adaptation refers to the process of increasing our fitness levels to adapt to a new cultural environment.

3. For most sojourners, they may experience culture shock in a sudden and abrupt way when they navigate a different cultural environment.

Unit 10　Intercultural Adaptation

4. Culture shock can bring about more problems than benefits.

_____

5. The only way to eliminate the problems caused by culture shock is to return to one's familiar surroundings.

_____

6. The U-curve and W-curve patterns are two popular models used to explain the developmental stages of intercultural adaptation.

_____

7. During the mastery stage of the U-curve pattern, sojourners won't experience anxiety and frustration any more, and have a better understanding of the host culture.

_____

III. Here are some postcards written by international students studying in China. Identify the stage of intercultural adaptation process for each student.

> honeymoon　　　crisis　　　adjustment　　　mastery

_____ period
Dear Joan,
　　Life here seems not so bad after all. The people are quite nice once you get to know them a little better and begin to figure out their way of looking at things. Guess I'm beginning to know the ropes.

Love,
Peter

_____ period
Dear Mum and Dad,
　　I'm really feeling fed up with my life here and longing for home. Getting anything done over here is a nightmare. The locals are so lazy and unhelpful. And on top of all that I feel down and sleepy all the time, seem to have lost all my zest.

Love,
Jim

_____ period

Dear Michael,

    This is a fantastic place! So many interesting things to see, such as the Forbidden City and the Temple of Heaven. Even wandering the streets is a delight with all the bustle and hordes of cyclists. I'm really happy I came.

Best wishes,
Simon

_____ period

Dear Nicky,

    Thanks for your letter. It was lovely to hear from you. I've been thinking about your question about what I find strangest about living in China, but the trouble is I've been here so long and have settled into the way of life so much that everything seems perfectly ordinary! So, if you want to find out, you'll have to come to see for yourself with a fresh pair of eyes. I can be your guide!

Best wishes,
Paul

Checking Basic Concepts

Complete the following statements with a proper word or phrase in the box. Each word or phrase can be used only once.

| culture shock | host culture | immigrant | intercultural adaptation |
| refugee | reverse culture shock | | sojourner |

1. The first time you travel abroad, you may experience a(n) _____.

2. Diplomats, international students, military personnel on foreign duty, business persons on assignment abroad, are called _____ who travel abroad for a long time, say one to five years, with the intent to return home.

3. A(n) _____ is a person who has come to live permanently in a country that is not native to them.

4. A(n) _____ is a person who has been forced to leave their country or home, because there is a war or for political, religious or social reasons.

5. When you travel abroad, learning about the history, tradition, language and even details such as food, music, transport, weather and social activities of your new _____ are all important.

6. According to Young Yun Kim, _____ is a long-term process of adjusting to and finally feeling comfortable in a new cultural environment.

7. It is possible to feel isolated and experience _____ when you return home after an extended period of time away.

Language in Use

I. Complete the following sentences with the words in the box. Change the form if necessary. Each word can be used only once.

| personnel | affective | hostility | symptom |
| distress | accommodate | incorporate | comprise |

1. The scandal (丑闻) in the newspaper caused the actor considerable _____.

2. One prominent _____ of the disease is the progressive loss of memory.

3. Administrative _____ should not only show leadership but also acquire some technical skills.

4. We have _____ all the latest safety features into the design.

5. _____ communication refers to how individual family members share their emotions with one another.

6. Although there is no overt _____, black and white students do not mix much.

7. I needed to _____ to the new schedule.

8. Older people _____ a large proportion of those living in poverty.

II. Paraphrase the following sentences from Text A.

1. Culture shock can be viewed as a transitional process in which sojourners gradually become aware of and begin to adjust to cultural differences in a new environment. This process may lead to either of two directions, depending on individual personality.

_____

_____

_____

2. Over the last few decades, scholars have tried to identify stages in the intercultural adaptation process. Among the research on this area, the U-curve and W-curve patterns are two popular models used to explain the developmental stages of intercultural adaptation.

_____

_____

 Expanding Intercultural Knowledge

Stress-Adaptation-Growth Dynamics

Young Yun Kim feels that cultural adjustment does not follow a strict U-curve pattern, but instead, it is a cyclical and continuous process. Unlike the U-curve pattern, Kim (2005) sees adaptation as an ongoing process in which sojourners continue to face and adapt to new challenges, following what Kim calls a Stress-Adaptation-Growth Dynamics pattern, as shown in the figure below.

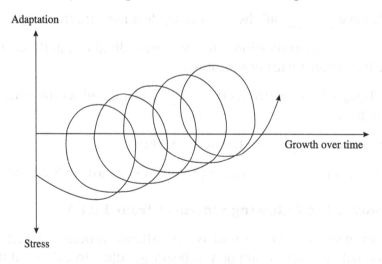

(Source: Kim, 2005)

Adjustment is cyclical, with increased adaptation over time, but in a "two-steps-forward-one-step-back", or a "draw-back-to-leap" pattern. Each stressful experience is responded with a "drawback" which, in turn, activates adaptive energy to help individuals reorganize themselves and "leap forward". This internal process reflects a dialectic relationship between new cultural learning (acculturation) and the unlearning of old cultural habits (deculturation). As sojourners work through the setbacks, they come out "victoriously", with an increased capacity to see others, themselves, and situations in a new light and to face challenges yet to come. Failure to work through this process results in prolonged feelings of inadequacy and frustration.

(Source: John R. Baldwin et al., *Intercultural Communication for Everyday Life*)

Reflecting and Discussing

Compare the U-curve pattern and the Stress-Adaptation-Growth Dynamics pattern. Which one do you think better describes and explains the development of intercultural adaptation? Why?

Adaptation Factors

Instructions: Imagine that you are going to a British university for graduate study. To evaluate your adaptation potential, rate yourself on the adaptation checklist. Give yourself a score for each item according to the following scale:

1 = Poor

2 = Not as good as most people

3 = Average

4 = Better than most people

5 = Excellent

Adaptation Checklist

Background and Preparation

_____ 1. Age—youth is an advantage.

_____ 2. Education—the higher, the better.

_____ 3. High level of professional skill.

_____ 4. General knowledge of the new culture, its history, customs, arts, etc.

_____ 5. Specific knowledge of the new situation, city, university, etc.

_____ 6. Oral and written fluency in the language of the new culture.

_____ 7. Previous out-of-culture experiences.

_____ 8. Similarity between home culture and new culture.

Personality Factors

_____ 9. Tends to be accepting of different ways of doing things.

_____ 10. Likes to meet new people and do new things.

_____ 11. Stays calm in difficult situations.

_____ 12. Pays attention to people and not just to tasks.

_____ 13. Can tolerate ambiguous or uncertain situations.

_____ 14. Has a sense of humor.

_____ 15. Strong but flexible in character.

_____ 16. Willing to take risks; not be too concerned about social and psychological security.

Attitudes and Motivation

_____ 17. Voluntarily choose to be in contact with the new culture.

_____ 18. Attracted to the new situation rather than escaping problems at home.

_____ 19. Admiration and respect for the new culture.

_____ 20. No sense that one culture is superior or inferior to another.

_____ 21. Few stereotypes about the new culture.

Health

_____ 22. Robust good health.

_____ 23. Good health habits.

_____ 24. High energy level.

_____ **Total score**

(Source: Linell Davis, *Doing Culture: Cross-Cultural Communication in Action*)

Unit 10   Intercultural Adaptation

Reflecting and Discussing

1. After you have completed the checklist, figure out what your advantages and disadvantages are in adapting to a new culture.

2. What can you do to increase your adaptation potential?

Strategies for Coping with Adaptation Stress

Do what you can to increase your score on the cultural adaptation checklist.

- You can't change your age, but you can learn more about your city or university and you can adjust your thinking.

Be alert for signs of adaptation stress.

- Health problems
- Loss of self-confidence
- Loneliness, sense of loss, severe homesickness
- Withdrawal from social contacts
- Negative feelings
- Behaving more aggressively than usual

Tell people at home what kind of support you really need from them.

- You may need freedom to make new decisions and their understanding of the difficulties you face more than you need their advice.

Use your "retreat" from the new culture constructively.

- Find home culture time and friends to refresh yourself and restore your positive feelings (speak your own language, eat family food, etc.).
- Look for people from your home country with positive attitudes.
- Don't spend time with people from home who reinforce negative feelings.

Pay attention to differences within the new culture.

- Avoid making broad generalizations about everybody in the host culture.

- Notice differences in background, motivation, personality; some people will be more like you than others.

- Just as you are not like everyone from your culture, so not everyone from the new culture is alike.

- People from the host culture may also be experiencing adaptation stress. When you are sensitive to their adaptation stress, you won't take their responses to you too personally.

Try to find two mentors (experienced helpers).

- Look for someone from your home culture who has more experience in the new culture than you do.

- Someone from the new culture with much experience with your culture.

- Consult your mentors to check your interpretations of cross-cultural events.

- Use your mentors to learn about hidden aspects of the new culture.

Seek out positive experiences within the new culture.

- If you like to watch football, watch football with people from the new culture.

- If you enjoy music, enjoy it with people from the new culture.

- That is, take your pleasures and relaxing activities into the new culture.

Be tolerant of yourself and others.

- Keep your sense of humor; misunderstandings can turn into funny stories.

- Assume that new culture associates (同伴) have reasons for their actions even if you do not understand them.

- Recognize that you are learning culture as you go through difficult experiences.

- If necessary, adjust your goals and time frame to make them more realistic.

Use your cross-cultural experience to increase your skills.

- Notice and imitate the communication styles of people from the new culture.

- Use concepts from cross-cultural communication studies to interpret your experience and adjust your behavior.

(Source: Linell Davis, *Doing Culture: Cross-Cultural Communication in Action*)

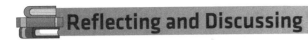

Unit 10 Intercultural Adaptation

Reflecting and Discussing

1. Using the list of strategies for coping with adaptation stress, give Wu Lian (see "Doubts" in the Lead-in section) advice about coping with her situation. Imagine her objections to your advice and try to find good answers for them.

2. Write an e-mail to Wu Lian's best friend at home explaining Wu Lian's present feelings and giving the friend some suggestions about how she can support Wu Lian while she is going through this difficult time.

Don't Be Afraid of Being Vulnerable

Read Text B and do the exercises online.

跨文化交际英语阅读教程
Intercultural Communication: An English Reading Coursebook

 Case Study

Discuss with your classmates the questions according to each case.

 Case 1

Culture Shock in Spain

This is a narration from Jessica Bahrke, an American student, for her intercultural experience in Spain.

When I moved to Madrid (马德里), I was on a high for about a month. Everything was new and exciting—the people, the food, the culture—everything was different and exhilarating (令人兴奋的). During this time, I took every opportunity to see the sights, visit museums, experience the never-ending night life, and eat as many tapas (西班牙小吃) as possible. This honeymoon period lasted for about four weeks before I really started to immerse myself in the Spanish culture. It took that long to realize that I was more or less living as a tourist on an extended vacation. In other words, it took about four weeks for the culture shock to sink in.

Before I left the States, I thought I had made every preparation I could to prevent culture shock. I honestly thought that I had mentally prepared myself and would be able to avoid the vast majority of the common struggles people go through when entering a new culture. I still feel as though my preparation allowed me to handle the shock better, but I was not able to avoid it altogether. A simple trip to the grocery store would leave me frustrated and upset. How could a country possibly survive without cooking spray? And, more importantly, how can I keep my eggs from sticking to the pan? Simple greeting practices also put me outside my comfort zone. Every time I met a new friend or acquaintance, I would extend my hand instinctually, expecting to feel a hand grips mine in return. Instead, I would be tugged (拽、拖) into an unexpected embrace and kissed once on each cheek before I realized what was going on. It wasn't as if I was unaware that this was customary in Europe—of course, I had read about this—but it always went against my nature to do it. Even though this introductory practice became commonplace, it never grew into a natural behavior during my time there.

(Source: James W. Neuliep, *Intercultural Communication: A Contextual Approach*)

1. How did Jessica feel at her first stage of intercultural adaptation? How long did this stage last for?

2. What problems and difficulties did she encounter at the second stage? How did she feel at this stage?

3. What advice would you give Jessica to help her cope with adaptation stress?

 Case 2

From Scotland to Canada

Ashley realized that she was a completely different person when she got back to Canada from Scotland.

After living in Edinburgh, Scotland for two years, I experienced a big dose of reverse culture shock when I moved back to Canada—which I wasn't expecting since the U.K. and Canada are similar in many ways.

But transitioning back to my old life, back to a place that was exactly the same as when I left it, was difficult. After living abroad, I had grown and changed irrevocably (无法挽回地) in so many ways, and I felt completely out of place when I returned. My hometown suddenly no longer felt like home.

I spent months feeling stressed and "homesick" for Edinburgh. Most of my friends aren't travelers and didn't understand what I was going through, so I felt completely alone and disconnected at times.

I've now been home for seven months and still don't feel like I've completely readjusted, but several things have helped ease the transition. Daily meditation, yoga, and gratitude exercises helped to reduce my stress levels and keep anxiety at bay.

Talking with like-minded people was reassuring, so I made an effort to connect with travelers and expats through blogs and Facebook groups.

The thing that helped me most when I moved home? Acceptance. Learning to accept the fact that I had changed and no longer felt like I belonged in my hometown—and that was okay.

(Source: Katherine Fenech, *From Scotland to Canada*)

1. What made Ashley's transition back to Canada from Edinburgh difficult? How did she feel about the transitioning experience?

2. What did she do to cope with her stress and readjust to the life back home?

References

Bai, J. Y. 2022. Don't Be Afraid of Being Vulnerable. Retrieved May 17, 2022, from Brown website.

Baldwin, J. R., Coleman, R. R. M., González, A. & Shenoy-Packer, S. 2014. *Intercultural Communication for Everyday Life*. West Sussex: Wiley-Blackwell.

Boroditsky, L. 2021. How Language Shapes the Way We Think. Retrieved Jun 20, 2022, from TED website.

Brick, J. 2004. *China: A Handbook in Intercultural Communication*. New Zealand: Macmillan Publishers.

Chang, J. Y., Lv, C. M. & Zhao, Y. Q. 2011. *Intercultural Communication*. Beijing: Peking University Press.

Chen, G. M. & Starosta, W. J. 2007. *Foundations of Intercultural Communication*. Shanghai: Shanghai Foreign Language Education Press.

Chinoy, S. 1996. Questions of Culture. Retrieved Sep 12, 2022, from bilibili website.

Davis, L. 2001. *Doing Culture: Cross-Cultural Communication in Action*. Beijing: Foreign Language Teaching and Research Press.

Dou, W. L. 2022. *Introduction to Intercultural Communication (The English Edition)* (3rd ed.). Beijing: International Business and Economics University Press.

Education World (no date). Eastern vs. Western Parenting. Retrieved Aug 14, 2022, from EducationWorld website.

Fan, W. W. 2009. *A Multimedia Approach to Intercultural Communication*. Beijing: Higher Education Press.

Fenech, K. 2018. From Scotland to Canada. Retrieved Jan 31, 2018, from Bright Lights of America website.

Ferrara, M. H. 2020. How and Why does Conflict Occur? Retrieved Jun 1, 2020, from Newsela website.

Hall. E. T. 1959. *The Silent Language*. New York: Doubleday.

Hofstede, G. & Hofstede, G. J. 2005. *Cultures and Organization: Software of the Mind* (2nd ed.). New York: McGraw-Hill.

Hou, H. Y. 2021. *Intercultural Reading: Appreciating Cultural Diversity*. Shanghai: East China Normal University Press.

Hu, C. 2006. *Intercultural Communication: A Practical Coursebook*. Beijing: Foreign Language Teaching and Research Press.

Huang, Y. C. 2016. *A New Comparison of English and Chinese Languages and Cultures*. Shanghai: Fudan University Press.

Jassen, C. 2023. How Ten Years in China Changed Me Forever. Retrieved May 20, 2023, from YouTube website.

Jia, Y. X. 2019. *Experiencing Global Intercultural Communication: Preparing for a Community of Shared Future for Mankind and Global Citizenship*. Beijing: Foreign Language Teaching and Research Press.

Kim, Y. Y. 2005. Adapting to a new culture: An integrative communication theory. In W. B. Gudykunst (Ed.), *Theorizing About Intercultural Communication*. Thousand Oaks: Sage, 375–400.

Kreuz, R. & Roberts, R. 2019. Understanding Personal Space Across Cultures. Retrieved Dec 22, 2019, from The MIT Press Reader website.

Liu, C. S. & Lee, H. W. 2008. A proposed model of expatriates in multinational organizations. *Cross-Cultural Management*, 15: 176–193.

Liu, Y. 2015. *East Meets West*. Cologne: Taschen.

Martin, J. N. & Nakayama, T. K. 2008. *Experiencing Intercultural Communication: An Introduction* (3rd ed.). New York: McGraw-Hill.

Martin, J. N. & Nakayama, T. K. 2010. *Intercultural Communication in Contexts*. New York: McGraw-Hill.

References

Neuliep, J. W. 2011. *Intercultural Communication: A Contextual Approach* (7th ed.). London: Sage.

Samovar, L. A., Porter, R. E., McDaniel, E. R. & Roy, C. S. 2013. *Communication Between Cultures* (8th ed.). Boston: Cengage Learning.

Samovar, L. A., Porter, R. E., McDaniel, E. R. & Roy, C. S. 2015. *Intercultural Communication: A Reader* (14th ed.). Boston: Cengage Learning.

Stevie, T. 2022. Body Language in Different Cultures. Retrieved Jul 21, 2023, from FluentU website.

The China Society for Human Rights Studies (CSHRS). 2022. Increasing Racial Discrimination Against Asians Exposes Overall Racist Nature of U.S. Society. Retrieved Apr 15, 2022, from Xinhua website.

Ting-Toomey, S. & Chung, L. C. 2012. *Understanding Intercultural Communication* (2nd ed.). New York: Oxford University Press.

Trosborg, A. (Ed.). 2010. *Pragmatics Across Languages and Cultures*. Berlin: Mouton de Gruyter.

Wang, R. & Zhang, A. L. 2018. *Bridge Between Minds: Intercultural Communication* (4th ed.). Chongqing: Chongqing University Press.

Xi, J. P. 2017. Work Together to Build the Silk Road Economic Belt and the 21st Century Maritime Silk Road. *China Daily*. Retrieved May 15, 2017, from Language Tips website.

Xu, C. W. 2020. *I Am Not Your Asian Stereotype*. Retrieved Feb 21, 2020, from bilibili website.

Xu, L. S. 2013. *Intercultural Communication in English* (rev ed.). Shanghai: Shanghai Foreign Language Education Press.

"清华社英语在线"(TUP English Online)平台使用指南

"清华社英语在线"集教、学、练、测、评、研等功能于一体,支持全媒体教学的泛在式外语学习。PC、移动端同步应用,提供互动式的教学环境、个性化的学习管理、多维度的学情监控、碎片化的应用场景,以实现混合式教学。平台基于数据设计,致力于全方位提高教学效率、提升教学效果、优化学习体验,为高校英语教师和学生提供在线学习、交流、教学管理、测试评估等服务。

一、数字课程使用指南

Step 1:登录平台(PC 端、移动端均可)

PC 端:www.tsinghuaelt.com(推荐使用 360 或 Google Chrome 浏览器);

移动端:微信内搜索小程序"清华社英语在线"或扫描下方小程序二维码。

Step 2:输入账号(登录账号、密码由平台创建)

(1)集体用户(学校教师统一授课)

由任课教师联系出版社,平台为学生统一创建登录账号。教师在平台开课后,学生进入教师课程学习;

（2）个人用户

登录界面点击【帮助中心】，联系平台在线客服获取账号密码，随后进入平台的公共课程内学习。

Step 3：激活课程（本书封底贴有教材配套验证码，输入以激活课程）

（1）进入教师课程后，点击【激活教材码】，刮开本书封底贴的激活码序列号并输入，即可激活课程开始学习；

（2）进入公共课程后，同上述方式激活课程后开始学习。

二、特别提示

1. 每本教材配套的激活码仅可在一个登录账号的配套课程中使用，激活成功后即失效，不可重复使用；

2. 激活码在成功激活课程后的使用期限为一年，请在开学初仅输入需要学习的课程的激活码；如因过早输入非本学期所学课程的激活码，导致课程届时过期而无法使用，我社不负责补发激活码；

3. 激活码遗失不补，需联系教师或自行购买新的教材或激活码。

三、帮助中心

数字课程及平台使用的常见问题，请在登录界面或课程内的【帮助中心–常见问题】处点击查看；如有其他疑问，请咨询平台在线客服。